306.85 FER

D1685344

C/21

Family&Parenthood
Policy&Practice

INVERNESS COLLEGE
LEARNING RESOURCE CENTRE
01463 273248

Parenting in the 1990s

Elsa Ferri and Kate Smith

PUBLISHED BY

Family Policy Studies Centre

SUPPORTED BY

JR
JOSEPH
ROWNTREE
FOUNDATION

Published by Family Policy Studies Centre
9 Tavistock Place, London WC1H 9SN
Tel: 0207 388 5900

ISBN 0 907051 98 7

November 1996 (eprinted September 1999)

© FPSC/JRF

The Family Policy Studies Centre is an independent body
which analyses family trends and the impact of policy. It is a
centre of research and information. The Centre's Governing
Council represents a wide spectrum of political opinion, as
well as professional, academic, faith, local authority and other
interests.

The Joseph Rowntree Foundation has supported this project as
part of its programme of research and innovative
development projects, which it hopes will be of value to policy
makers and practitioners. The facts presented and views
expressed in this report, however, are those of the authors
and not necessarily those of the Foundation.

Design and print by Intertype

Contents

Note

Tables and figures contained in this Report are numbered sequentially in the text (Table 1, Table 2 etc). Other tables referred to in the text, eg. Table 2.1, Table 3.4, are not published here but are obtainable upon request from the authors at the Social Statistics Research Unit, City University.

List of tables

List of figures

Acknowledgements

Our thanks are due to the Joseph Rowntree Foundation who funded this study, and also to the members of our Advisory Group – Barbara Ballard, Julia Brannen, Louie Burghes, Erica De'ath, Susan McRae, Penny Mansfield and Barbara Maughan – for their support and comments throughout the project.

We should also like to express our gratitude to the members of the National Child Development Study cohort who have continued over many years to participate in this longitudinal study and give of their time to provide information about themselves and their lives. Without their continuing co-operation this, and a great many other studies based on the NCDS data, would not be possible.

Elsa Ferri and Kate Smith
Social Statistics Research Unit
City University
London

1963; Davie *et al.*, 1972; Fogelman, 1976; Wedge, 1969). The latest survey, in 1991, when the cohort were aged 33, added to this wealth of data extensive new information about them, by means of personal interviews and self-completion questionnaires (Ferri, 1993). The research reported here is based largely on this new data. Of particular relevance were details of partnerships and family formation; employment and income; child-care arrangements and other parenting behaviour; family activities and relationships; and social attitudes and values. For a one-in-three sample, wide-ranging data were also obtained about the characteristics and development of their children. This breadth of coverage of the 1991 NCDS survey enabled many of these questions relating to parenting to be addressed. Combined with earlier sweeps, it provided a three-generation dataset, which meant that the parenting behaviour of the cohort members could also be compared with that of their own fathers and mothers.

Parents in NCDS

The early 30s are an important stage in the life cycle from the point of view of family formation and working life. Most people by this age have completed their education and training, established their position in the labour market, set up independent households and made the transitions to partnership and parenthood. However, it is also a period at which pressures relating to work and family life are likely, for many, to be at a maximum, with regard to career advancement, the financial costs of housing, the needs of young dependent children, and so on. It is a key point, therefore, at which to investigate patterns of parenting and family life.

Three-quarters (77%) of the women and two-thirds (66%) of the men in the NCDS cohort had become parents by the age of 33. Almost all of the mothers (97%), and the great majority (85%) of the fathers had all their children living with them at the time of the survey (Ferri, 1993). The lower figure for fathers reflects the likelihood that children remain in the care of the mother when relationships break down. Linked to this, a higher proportion of men (11%) than women (2%) were bringing up children who were not their biological offspring, reflecting the fact that reconstituted families mostly include step*fathers* rather than step*mothers*.

Of the cohort fathers who had all their children living with them, practically all (99%) were living with a partner, and 90% were in a first marriage.

The remainder were equally divided between those in second or subsequent marriages, and cohabiting partnerships. The picture for the cohort mothers was rather different: 89% were with a partner, and 73% in first marriages. Like the fathers, the others were evenly split between the remarried (9%) and cohabiting (7%). However, 11% of mothers, compared to just 1% of fathers, were lone parents at the time of the survey. (Further analysis of the partnership and parenthood situations of the cohort members can be found in Ferri and Smith, forthcoming(a)).

Since our study was concerned with *parental couples*, and how they managed their work and family lives, those bringing up children on their own were not included. Also, it was decided to leave out cohabiting couples and those in stepfamilies, since other research has shown that these differ in many relevant respects from married couples and parents caring for only the children of their partnership (Ferri, 1984; Kiernan and Estaugh, 1993). Our study, therefore, focused on married couples and the children born to that union. The sample included almost 6000 cases: 2800 fathers and 3192 mothers, representing approximately 76% and 72% respectively of all NCDS fathers and mothers. These figures indicate that, although only a minority of British *households* now consist of a married couple and their children, and while a considerable diversity of family forms was found among the NCDS cohort in 1991, the 'traditional' nuclear family remained the norm among those who were parents at age 33.

The majority of the parents in the study (54% of

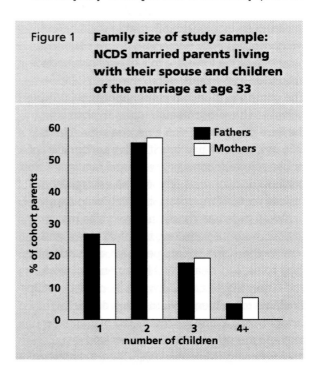

Figure 1 **Family size of study sample: NCDS married parents living with their spouse and children of the marriage at age 33**

fathers and 55% of mothers) had two children (Figure 1). Large families of four or more children were uncommon, involving just 4% of fathers and 5% of mothers. It is important to bear in mind, of course, that, at the age of 33, many of the cohort members would not have completed their families. The children concerned ranged in age from early infancy to just one 17-year-old.

It is important to make clear that the unit of analysis in the study was the NCDS cohort member, i.e. a father *or* a mother. These fathers and mothers, therefore, were not married to *each other;* as far as possible their partners, who were not members of the NCDS cohort, are referred to as wives and husbands respectively.

In the following chapter, we investigate the links between work and family life among the mothers and fathers in the study and, in Chapter 3, how their employment patterns related to the ways they organised the care of children and other domestic responsibilities. Chapter 4 looks more closely at the home setting, in terms of the time spent by the family members in joint activities, and at parenting practice in relation to child-rearing. In Chapter 5, we examine how different patterns of parenting related to the quality of the relationship between the couples, their overall satisfaction with their lives, and their self-assessed mental health. The final chapter considers the implications of the study's findings, and ways in which more effective support might be provided to those undertaking the challenging task of parenting in the 1990s.

Paid work

This chapter highlights the diverse employment contexts in which the NCDS parents were bringing up their children. Most of these mothers and fathers, who were aged 33 in 1991, would have made the transition to parenthood during the 1980s, a period of considerable changes in the labour market, which had important consequences for the care and raising of children. Most significant among these was the continuing increase in the proportions of mothers in paid work, while high male unemployment and the moves to a 'flexible' labour market also had a major impact on families and parenting (Brannen et al., 1994).

As has become the norm among British couples generally, the dual earner household was the most common combination among the NCDS parents, although, also in line with the overall pattern, families in which the mother worked part-time were more than twice as numerous as those with two full-time workers. Parents in the dual full-time earner homes differed from those with a part-time working mother by having relatively high qualifications, high status occupations and smaller families. They were also strikingly better off financially than any other group. Those in the 'traditional' single earner families, with only the father in employment, resembled the dual full-time earners in educational and social background, but a much higher proportion had very young children. At the other end of the spectrum were parents in households with no earner. They were characterised by a lack of educational qualifications, low status of previous occupation, large families, relatively early parenthood, and, most of all, economic disadvantage. The small group of families in which the *mother* was the sole earner was also concentrated in the low income group.

Largely irrespective of their wives' employment situation, or the number and ages of their children, the cohort fathers spent long hours at work, and, for the majority, their jobs involved working in the evenings and at weekends. The employment situation of mothers, on the other hand, was strongly linked to how many children they had, and

whether they were under school age. In contrast to fathers, most mothers worked relatively short hours, while a substantial minority of mothers, too, had evening, night or weekend jobs.

Couples' employment situations

The great majority (94%) of the cohort fathers were in employment in 1991, and virtually all were working full-time (Table 2.1). More than three-quarters (77%) were employees and one in seven (16%) were self-employed. Four per cent of fathers indicated that they were unemployed and just 1% were sick or disabled.

Nearly two-thirds (62%) of the cohort mothers were employed, 19% full-time and 43% part-time. Self-employment was less common than among the fathers: just 7% of mothers were in this category, while 55% were employees. Most of the remaining mothers (35%) were 'looking after home and family'; the rest were categorised as unemployed, in full-time education, or sick/disabled (about 1% in each case).

Our main interest, however, was in the *combined* employment situations of the cohort mothers and fathers and their respective partners. Here, the findings revealed marked contrasts in the circumstances in which these parents were raising their families. Fifty-nine per cent of mothers and 53% of fathers were in *dual earner* households, echoing the findings of other recent surveys which indicate that this has become the dominant pattern in contemporary Britain (Brannen et al., 1994). The most common combination within this group was for fathers to be working full-time and mothers part-time: in fewer than one in five of all couples (18% of mothers and 15% of fathers) were both parents in full-time employment (Figure 2 and Table 2.2).

The *single earner* household, as represented by the 'traditional' combination of working father and home-based mother, accounted for 41% of the cohort fathers and 34% of the mothers. In a small minority of cases (2% of fathers and 3% of mothers) the mother was the family's sole earner.

The final category of combined employment

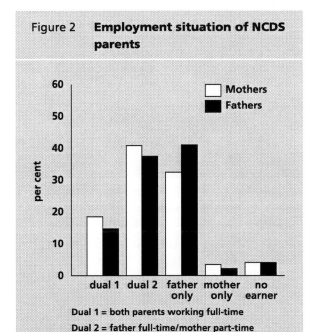

Figure 2   Employment situation of NCDS parents

Dual 1 = both parents working full-time
Dual 2 = father full-time/mother part-time

situations was the *no earner* household, accounting for 4% of both mothers and fathers. In the great majority of these cases, the father was reported to be unemployed and the mother as 'looking after home or family'.

These findings confirm those of other studies which have shown that the employment situations of household partners are related, and that it is this which has contributed to the growing polarisation into 'work rich' and 'work poor'

households (Gregg and Wadsworth, 1995). Employed fathers were much more likely to have working wives (57%) than those who were out of the labour market (31%) (Table 2.2). Similarly, the employment rate for cohort mothers with working husbands (64%) was much higher than that for mothers whose husbands were unemployed, or otherwise out of the labour market (41%).

A link between the *self-employed* status of the couples was also revealed. Twelve per cent of self-employed fathers had wives who were also self-employed, compared with just 4% of employee fathers (Table 2.3). Among the mothers, no fewer than 42% of those who were themselves self-employed had self-employed husbands, as against just 15% of employee mothers. We were not able to explore the work situations of these couples any further at this stage, but it seems likely that in many of these cases both parents were involved in a 'family' enterprise.

The dual earner family

There were striking differences within the *dual earner* groups according to whether the mother/wife worked full-time or part-time. Couples who were both full-time earners were twice as likely *both* to be in professional or managerial jobs (27% among cohort fathers and cohort mothers) as those in which the mother worked part-time (12% and 13% respectively, Table 1). In the latter

Table 1   Combined social class of occupation among parents in dual earner families

cohort fathers	wife working:	
	full-time %	part-time %
both professional/managerial	27	12
father professional/ managerial, wife non-manual	10	13
father professional/ managerial, wife manual	7	8
wife professional/managerial, father non-manual	4	3
wife professional/managerial, father manual	14	11
both non-manual	5	5
father non-manual, wife non-manual	3	4
father manual, wife non-manual	14	19
both manual	16	24
total	**100**	**100**
(n)	**(400)**	**(968)**

cohort mothers	mother working:	
	full-time %	part-time %
both professional/managerial	27	13
mother professional/ managerial, husband non-manual	5	3
mother professional/ managerial, husband manual	14	10
husband professional/managerial, mother non-manual	8	14
husband professional/managerial, mother manual	6	9
both non-manual	4	5
mother non-manual, husband non-manual	14	19
mother manual, husband non-manual	2	4
both manual	19	24
total	**100**	**100**
(n)	**(542)**	**(1227)**

group, both mothers *and* fathers were more likely to be in lower status occupations: in 24% of cases both partners were in manual jobs. These findings are in line with data from the Labour Force Survey on mothers in full- and part-time work (Brannen and Moss, 1991). Couples who both worked full-time also tended to have higher educational qualifications. This was especially marked among the cohort mothers: 41% of full-time workers had A-levels or higher compared with just 30% of those in part-time work (Table 2). This difference is also consistent with those found in other national datasets such as the General Household Survey (Bridgwood and Savage, 1993). In view of this, and their relatively high occupational status, it was not surprising that the dual full-time earner families were also by far the most affluent group. Exactly half of both the fathers and the mothers in this situation had a total weekly household income in the top quartile of the overall distribution, compared with just one in five of those in which the mother worked part-time (Figure 3 (b)).

Interestingly, the educational qualifications of mothers in part-time work were almost identical to those of their home-based peers, yet the most *recent* jobs held by the latter group were of a much higher occupational status than the *current* posts of the part-time working mothers (Table 2.4). This may be indicative of the limited job opportunities open to mothers who choose, or are obliged, to work part-time. In economic terms, the main effect of part-time maternal employment appeared to be to lift the family out of the lowest income category: only half as many such families fell in the bottom quartile as those in which the

father was the sole earner (17% and 33% respectively among cohort fathers; 16% versus 30% among cohort mothers). These findings would seem to illustrate the economic pressures on many families for both parents to engage in paid employment (see page 8 above).

A number of studies have shown that family size is related to parental employment situation (Brannen *et al.*, 1994). This was also the case among the NCDS dual earner families: those in which both parents worked full-time were twice as likely to have just one child as those in which the mother worked part-time (44% as against 23% among cohort fathers; 40% and 18% respectively among cohort mothers: Table 3).

The age of the children concerned made much less difference to the full/part-time split. Among the fathers, there was no difference between those with full- and part-time working wives in the number with a youngest child under school age (59% in each case), while among mothers the respective figures were 46% and 50% (Table 4). It is likely that this similarity in the age structure of the children of full- and part-time working mothers in the NCDS cohort reflects recent trends for more highly educated women to have children later, and to take advantage of maternity leave legislation to return sooner to full-time, higher status jobs (e.g. Harrop and Moss, 1994; McRae and Daniel, 1991: Macran *et al.*, 1995). The high proportion of dual earner families with pre-school children has, of course, important implications for child care and the provision of appropriate support services, which we examine later.

Table 2	Parents' highest educational qualification, by couple's employment situation					

cohort fathers:	dual earner:		single earner:		no earner	all
	wife ft	wife pt	wife home	wife works		
	%	%	%	%	%	%
none	11	9	8	22	40	10
some/O level	40	47	38	35	36	42
A level/higher	36	35	37	33	19	35
degree	13	9	17	10	5	13
total	100	100	100	100	100	100
(n)	(417)	(1022)	(1051)	(46)	(80)	(2616)

cohort mothers:	dual earner:		single earner:		no earner	all
	mother ft	mother pt	mother home	mother works		
	%	%	%	%	%	%
none	9	11	11	20	52	12
some/O level	49	60	58	50	46	56
A level/higher	27	22	21	24	2	22
degree	14	8	10	6	—	10
total	100	100	100	100	100	100
(n)	(551)	(1274)	(971)	(70)	(95)	(2961)

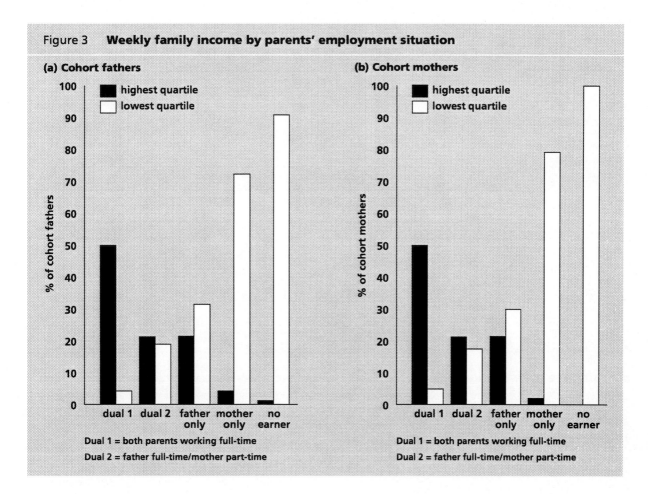

Figure 3   Weekly family income by parents' employment situation

(a) Cohort fathers

% of cohort fathers

- ■ highest quartile
- □ lowest quartile

dual 1   dual 2   father only   mother only   no earner

Dual 1 = both parents working full-time
Dual 2 = father full-time/mother part-time

(b) Cohort mothers

% of cohort mothers

- ■ highest quartile
- □ lowest quartile

dual 1   dual 2   father only   mother only   no earner

Dual 1 = both parents working full-time
Dual 2 = father full-time/mother part-time

Table 3   Parental employment situation and number of children in the family

cohort fathers:	dual earner:		single earner:		no earner
	wife ft	wife pt	wife home	wife works	
	%	%	%	%	%
no. of children:					
1	44	23	23	31	13
2	47	60	53	48	44
3	8	14	19	17	31
4 +	1	3	5	4	13
total	**100**	**100**	**100**	**100**	**100**
(n)	**(428)**	**(1046)**	**(1069)**	**(46)**	**(87)**

cohort mothers:	dual earner:		single earner:		no earner
	mother ft	mother pt	mother home	mother works	
	%	%	%	%	%
no. of children:					
1	40	18	19	19	12
2	47	62	53	57	38
3	11	18	22	18	28
4 +	2	2	6	6	22
total	**100**	**100**	**100**	**100**	**100**
(n)	**(564)**	**(1293)**	**(987)**	**(70)**	**(96)**

Table 4

Table 4   Parental employment situation and age of youngest child

cohort fathers:	dual earner:		single earner:		no
	wife ft	wife pt	wife home	wife works	earner
	%	%	%	%	%
age of youngest:					
under 5	59	59	84	54	57
5 - 10	36	39	16	37	39
11 and over	5	2	<1	9	4
total	**100**	**100**	**100**	**100**	**100**
(n)	**(426)**	**(1045)**	**(1068)**	**(46)**	**(87)**

cohort mothers:	dual earner:		single earner:		no
	mother ft	mother pt	mother home	mother works	earner
	%	%	%	%	%
age of youngest:					
under 5	46	50	77	46	49
5 - 10	44	45	23	47	46
11 and over	10	5	1	7	5
total	**100**	**100**	**100**	**100**	**100**
(n)	**(563)**	**(1293)**	**(986)**	**(70)**	**(96)**

The single earner family

Fathers who were *single earners* were very similar to their peers in dual full-time worker households in terms of their social class of occupation (45% in both cases were in professional/managerial jobs (Table 5). As far as educational background was concerned, however, single earner fathers were the group most likely to have high qualifications: 17% were graduates compared with 13% of those with full-time working wives and just 9% of those whose wives worked part-time (Table 2). It seems likely that the higher qualifications of the single earner fathers were associated with greater earning power, and consequently less economic pressure for their wives to be in employment. However, in terms of weekly household income, while these families had a similar proportion in the top quartile of the distribution to those in which the mother worked part-time, they were twice as likely to be in the *lowest* income category (Figure 3). The fact that as many as one in three families with only the father in employment were in the bottom income quartile underlines the importance of two earned incomes for a satisfactory standard of living.

Families in which only the father was in the labour market were rather larger than those in which the mother worked part-time (among cohort fathers, 24% and 17% respectively had three or more children, while among mothers the

Table 5   Cohort members' social class of occupation, by couple's employment status

cohort fathers:	dual earner:		single earner:	all
	wife ft	wife pt	wife home	
	%	%	%	%
professional	8	5	9	7
managerial	37	28	36	33
skilled non-manual	12	12	13	12
skilled manual	27	37	31	33
semi skilled/unskilled	16	18	11	15
total	**100**	**100**	**100**	**100**
(n)	**(410)**	**(998)**	**(1027)**	**(2435)**

cohort mothers:	dual earner:		single earner:	all
	mother ft	mother pt	mother home	
	%	%	%	%
professional	2	2	—	2
managerial	44	24	21	30
skilled non-manual	26	37	27	34
skilled manual	8	6	14	7
semi skilled/unskilled	20	31	38	28
total	**100**	**100**	**100**	**100**
(n)	**(557)**	**(1259)**	**(66)**	**(1882)**

Parenting in the 1990s

figures were 28% and 20%: Table 3). What particularly distinguished these single earner families, however, was the large number with children under school age: 84% of the cohort fathers and 77% of the cohort mothers – a much higher proportion than in any other employment group (Table 4). Thus, while the mothers in these families may have *chosen* to be at home, the size and age structure of their families also meant that finding substitute day care would be an obstacle to taking up employment.

The characteristics of the small group of families in which the *mother* was the sole earner contrasted sharply to the 'traditional' situation just described. A relatively high proportion of these employed cohort mothers had no qualifications (20%: Table 2), as was the case among unemployed cohort fathers whose wives were sole earners (22%). Sole earner mothers were more likely than others to be in manual occupations (52% compared with 37% of part-time workers: Table 5), while the occupational status of the most *recent* job held by unemployed *fathers* in this group was also relatively low (Table 2.4). These 'role reversal' families did not differ from the 'traditional' single earner families in terms of the number of children in the household (Table 3), but they were much less likely to have a child under five – a factor which would facilitate the mothers' participation in the labour market (Table 4).

Given the concentration of single earner mothers in low status occupations, it was not surprising that the great majority of these families fell into the bottom quartile on household income: 74% of cohort fathers' families and 79% of cohort mothers' (Figure 3). This reinforces the point made by other analysts (e.g. Condy and Roberts, 1995) that, while women's part-time employment may lift families out of poverty, it is unlikely to provide an adequate standard of living if the male partner is out of work.

The no earner family

The families which contrasted most with the others in terms of background characteristics were those with *no earner* in the household. The picture which emerged was one of multiple disadvantage. No fewer than 40% of cohort fathers and 52% of cohort mothers in this group had no formal educational qualifications (Table 2). This compared with just 11% and 14% respectively among all men and women in the NCDS cohort (Bynner and Fogelman, 1993). Among the fathers, 36% had been in semi- or

unskilled occupations in their most recent job – twice as many as in any other group (Table 2.4). The picture for the cohort mothers in no earner families was even more striking: 59% had last worked in a semi- or unskilled job, compared with just 20% of those with husbands currently employed. Unsurprisingly, the most striking characteristic of these families was economic disadvantage, with virtually all falling into the lowest quartile of income distribution (100% of cohort mothers and 93% of cohort fathers) (Figure 3).

These findings all point to the weak labour market position of these parents, which was further emphasised by the fact that they were the group with the largest families. Thirteen per cent of the fathers had four or more children, compared with a mere 1% of those in dual full-time worker families; while the corresponding figures for mothers were 22% and 2% (Table 3). This means, of course, that, while the no earner family is a relatively small group, a disproportionately large number of *children* suffer from the deprivations associated with parents' exclusion from the labour force (Kiernan and Wicks, 1990; Kumar, 1993). The plight of such families is compounded by the fact that having a large number of children tends to make it difficult for poorly qualified parents to find work which would offer a viable economic alternative to welfare dependency.

The no earner families had also become parents at a relatively early age. It is important to remember that the NCDS sample were all 33 years old in 1991, and that the age distribution of their children thus reflected the age at which they became parents. Thirty per cent of the fathers and 52% of the mothers in the no earner households had an eldest child aged 11 or over; that is, they had had their first child at age 22 or younger (Table 2.5). Other studies (e.g. Kiernan, 1995; Payne, 1987) have also found that early parenthood is adversely related to career and economic prospects, and is more likely to be experienced by those who themselves grew up in disadvantaged circumstances and were less successful at school.

Parents' working hours

How long parents are at work, and when, is important in terms of the time available for parenting and family life. British men have the longest working hours in Europe (Eurostat, 1992), and the NCDS fathers were at a stage in the life cycle when their commitment to the labour market was likely to be at a maximum (European Community Childcare Network, 1993). The 1991 NCDS survey confirmed this picture: two-thirds of the cohort fathers worked 40 or more hours a week, over a quarter 50 or more, and nearly 1 in 10 worked 60+ hours (Figure 4(a)).

Overall, *single earner* fathers were the most likely to work long hours. However, social class of occupation was also a significant factor. Long (50+) hours were most common among fathers in managerial and skilled manual occupations. The hours worked by fathers in managerial jobs did not vary according to their wives' employment situation, but those in semi- and unskilled manual occupations were less likely to work long hours if their wives were also employed (Table 2.6). It may be that manual workers whose wives were also in the labour market forfeited maximising their own earnings through overtime. For fathers in managerial positions, however, the demands of the job, or their own career aspirations, may have led to them working long hours regardless of their partners' employment situation. The number and ages of the children in the family was also found to be unrelated to fathers' working hours (Tables 2.7 and 2.8).

As well as the total number of hours, we also looked at what part of the day parents worked. In the 1990s labour market terminology, 'flexible' has tended to replace 'unsocial' in describing shiftwork, or other than normal daytime working. The latter term may be more appropriate, however, in relation to the impact of such arrangements on family life.

Working outside normal hours affected the *majority* of the cohort fathers: two-thirds worked in the evenings, and six out of ten at weekends (Table 6). Almost a third worked at night, between

10pm and 4am, and rather more than this between 4 am and 7am. Predictably, the extra working hours of fathers in professional, managerial and other non-manual jobs were more likely to be in the evenings, while more manual workers worked at night or at weekends (Table 2.9). Family characteristics, in terms of the number and ages of their children, showed little relationship to fathers' unsocial hours (Tables 2.10 and 2.11), and there was no link at all with their wives' employment situation. This last finding suggests, therefore, that for many families in which the mother worked *and* the father worked unsocial hours, the time available for both parents to be together in the family would be considerably reduced.

In contrast to British men, women in this country work shorter hours than almost all of their European neighbours (European Commission Childcare Network, 1993). Furthermore, mothers tend to work fewer hours than their childless counterparts (Dex *et al.*, 1993). This polarisation of the hours worked by British mothers and fathers was also observable among the NCDS parents. Only a quarter of the cohort mothers worked more than 35 hours a week, and as many as one in three did fewer than 16 hours (Figure 4 (b)). The small group of professional mothers were the most likely to work 35 hours or more (39%), followed by those in managerial positions (34%: Table 2.12). By contrast, nearly half of those in semi- or unskilled jobs worked less than 16 hours a week.

In contrast to fathers, family characteristics made a considerable difference to mothers' working patterns. Having a second child doubled the number of mothers who worked fewer than 16 hours, from 18% to 35% (Table 2.7). The age of the

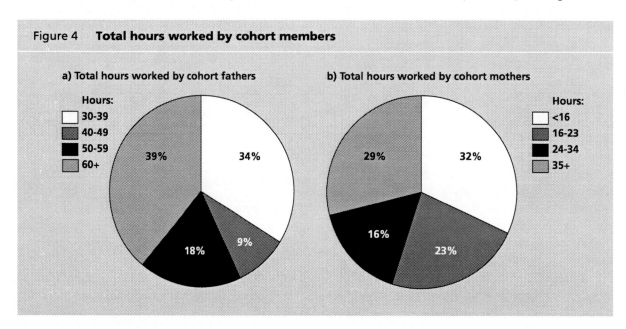

Figure 4   **Total hours worked by cohort members**

a) Total hours worked by cohort fathers

Hours:
30-39
40-49
50-59
60+

39%   34%   9%   18%

b) Total hours worked by cohort mothers

Hours:
<16
16-23
24-34
35+

29%   32%   16%   23%

Table 6   Number of parents working unsocial hours, by couple's employment situation

cohort fathers:	dual earner: mother ft	dual earner: mother pt	single earner: father only	all
	%	%	%	%
evenings (6 pm - 10 pm)	67	63	67	65
nights (10 pm - 4 am)	36	30	31	31
nights (4 am - 7 am)	38	36	37	37
weekends	60	61	58	60
(approx n)	**(318)**	**(846)**	**(843)**	**(2037)**

cohort mothers:	dual earner: mother ft	dual earner: mother pt	single earner: mother only	all
	%	%	%	%
evenings (6 pm - 10 pm)	43	37	42	38
nights (10 pm - 4 am)	17	15	17	16
nights (4 am - 7 am)	15	10	18	12
weekends	39	39	43	39
(approx n)	**(449)**	**(1121)**	**(60)**	**(1630)**

children made rather less difference, although having a child under five was also associated with mothers working short (under 16) hours (Table 2.8).

Overall, four out of ten mothers worked in the evening or at the weekend, one in six worked at night between 10pm and 4am, and one in eight did early morning shifts (4am to 7am) (Table 6). The proportion of mothers working 'unsocial' hours increased slightly with each rise in the number of children (Table 2.10). Those with children under school age were also more likely to work in the evenings than those whose families were older. It would seem, then, that working unsocial hours is a relatively common phenomenon among mothers with the most demanding family responsibilities. Martin and Roberts (1984) also found that women with children were more likely than others to work either early in the morning or late in the evening, when husbands were available to provide child care.

The above findings reflect those of other data sources which show the contrasting hours worked by fathers and mothers. However, they also fit in with other evidence which has indicated that family circumstances have little effect on fathers' working time, whereas the ways in which mothers participate in the labour market is largely determined by their prime responsibility for family life (e.g. Gershuny, 1995; Henwood *et al.*, 1987).

Intergenerational patterns of maternal employment

Before leaving this topic, we look briefly at the unique information provided by NCDS on

Table 7   Cohort mother's employment situation, by whether own mother worked

	dual earner: mother ft	dual earner: mother pt	single earner: mother home	single earner: mother works	no earner	all
a) before started school:	%	%	%	%	%	%
own mother worked - ft	12	8	8	10	7	8
own mother worked - pt	33	22	19	27	15	21
own mother did not work	66	70	74	63	78	71
total	**100**	**100**	**100**	**100**	**100**	**100**
(n)	**(472)**	**(1114)**	**(840)**	**(62)**	**(73)**	**(2561)**
b) after started school:						
own mother worked - ft	14	10	8	10	13	10
own mother worked - pt	35	36	33	45	31	35
own mother did not work	51	54	58	45	56	55
total	**100**	**100**	**100**	**100**	**100**	**100**
(n)	**(485)**	**(1144)**	**(851)**	**(62)**	**(78)**	**(2620)**
c) between 7 and 11:						
own mother worked	66	63	59	66	57	62
own mother did not work	34	37	41	34	43	38
total	**100**	**100**	**100**	**100**	**100**	**100**
(n)	**(474)**	**(1088)**	**(851)**	**(61)**	**(68)**	**(2540)**

intergenerational patterns of employment. Since a major change in the labour market in the intervening years concerned maternal employment, our main interest was in any link between the cohort mothers' labour market experience and that of their own mothers. Did working mothers produce working daughters?

Three measures from earlier surveys were of relevance here, namely, whether the cohort member's mother had worked before and/or after the child started school and between the ages of seven and eleven.

The first point to note is that, despite the intervening increase in maternal employment rates, having a working mother had, in fact, been a common experience in the cohort members' families of origin. Nearly three out of ten had worked before the cohort member started school, almost half by the time the child was seven, and nearly two-thirds in the four years between the seven- and eleven-year surveys (Table 7).

What was most interesting, however, was the slight, but consistent, link between the work pattern of the cohort mothers and that of their own mothers. Those who were employed full-time in dual earner families, and those who were the sole earners in their households, were the most likely to have had working mothers themselves (45% and 37% respectively before they had started school). Conversely, those least likely to have experienced maternal employment were the mothers currently out of the labour market (27%). Clearly, the employment behaviour of the cohort mothers will have been determined by a complex range of factors, including their present family circumstances and personal characteristics. However, these findings also point to some influence of parental role models in their decisions concerning their own working lives.

Home, work and family roles

We now turn to unpaid work, and in particular to how the care and upbringing of children were shared between the couples in the different employment groups. What relationship was there between parents' working lives and the way their family lives were organised? Was there any connection between the parenting arrangements they had adopted and what they themselves had experienced as children?

The findings showed that the couples' employment situation, and, for fathers in particular, their working hours, were reflected to a considerable extent in the division of child care and domestic work. In general, the more mothers were involved in the labour market, the more fathers participated in parenting and household tasks. However, the mother's major responsibility for domestic life remained, especially when this demanded parental *time*, as in the care of sick children. When fathers worked more than 50 hours a week, their contribution was sharply reduced, irrespective of their wives' employment status. Regardless of the mothers' work situation, too, highly educated fathers, and those in professional and managerial positions, showed relatively low involvement in child care.

Despite these varying levels of paternal involvement, it was none the less the case that fathers, as well as grandparents and other informal sources, were the main source of child care for working mothers. Employer-provided child care was virtually unreported, and only a tiny minority of parents made use of formal educational or day-care provision.

Care arrangements for children of working parents

We look first at the actual care arrangements made by employed parents when they were at work. Who provided this, and to what extent was support for child care furnished by sources, either formal or informal, outside the immediate family?

Unfortunately, this question was put only to *female* cohort members who were employed and who had children under 14 – a research design element which reveals a distinctly traditional view of child care as the sole concern of mothers. Employed mothers were shown a lengthy list of child-care sources and asked 'What are your usual arrangements for looking after the children when you are at work?'.

The most striking finding was the major contribution of family members – especially husbands, parents and in-laws – a picture very much in line with other recent studies in this area (Marsh and McKay, 1993). Irrespective of the age of the children involved, well over a third of the mothers said that their husbands provided child care, and almost as many indicated that grandparents did so (Table 8).

For those with pre-school children, no form of public provision came anywhere near the role played by the family. The main formal source of care was child-minders, used by about one in six parents. Of the other day-care services which correspond to parents' working hours, only private day nurseries were used by a sizeable minority: 8%. Only 10 of the 906 mothers concerned had a place in a local authority day nursery, no doubt reflecting the fact that the latter are almost exclusively reserved for high-need families (Ferri, 1992). Nursery schools and playgroups were each used by 6% of parents, although it is unlikely that the short hours normally offered by such provision fully met the child-care needs of even the part-time working mothers. Despite the much-heralded developments of the 1980s, just 15 mothers had work-place child care. Governmental anticipation that employers would step in to meet the shortfall in provision – made even more acute by the policy of encouraging mothers into the workforce – appears to have resulted in neither a substantial, nor an appropriate, solution to the problem (Cohen, 1988; Moss, 1990; Working for Childcare, 1990).

Packages of care

The various sources of care were combined into three groups: *husbands, informal care* (parents or

Table 8   Working cohort mothers: numbers using each type of child care by age of youngest child

	Age of youngest child:		
	under 5	5 or over	total
children cared for by:	%	%	%
husband	37	36	36
parents/in-laws	35	34	35
other relatives	7	9	8
friends	8	10	9
neighbours	2	4	3
live-in nanny/au pair	<1	<1	<1
other nanny/au-pair	4	<1	2
registered childminder	17	4	10
unregistered childminder	2	2	2
play group	6	<1	3
workplace nursery	2	<1	1
LA day nursery	1	<1	1
private day nursery	8	<1	4
out of school club	<1	<1	<1
nursery school/class	6	<1	3
infant/primary school	19	45	32
secondary school	1	13	7
old enough to care for themselves	<1	5	3
other arrangement	7	7	7
no usual arrangement	1	4	3
total with information (n)	**(906)**	**(956)**	**(1862)**

Note: the above figures do not necessarily indicate that the care arrangement mentioned applies to the youngest child (eg 12 mothers with youngest child under 5 answered 'secondary school', which would relate to an older child in the family).

in-laws, other relatives, friends or neighbours) and *formal care* (day care or education provision).

This showed that fathers, either alone or in combination with other sources, provided care in four out of ten cases where the youngest child was under five, and in half of those with over-fives only (Table 9). In the latter group, paternal care was most likely to be combined with other *informal* care – that is, from parents, relatives or friends; where there were pre-school children, it was most often the sole source. The pattern also varied, however, according to both the fathers' own job situations and the mothers' working hours.

In the *dual earner* households, paternal care was most common when the mother worked very short (less than 16) hours a week. Among those with under-fives in this group, 54% of husbands looked after the children, and were sole carers in 37% of cases. Where the oldest child was over five, husbands provided child care in 65% of cases, and, again, were the sole providers in 37%. As nearly all these fathers were themselves working full-time, it would seem that, especially when they provided sole care, 'shift parenting' operated in many families. Indeed, in 71% of cases, the mother concerned worked in the evening between 6pm and 10pm. When mothers worked longer (35+) hours, fathers figured less in

the care arrangements – just 19% in families with under-fives and 39% in those with school age children. However, great reliance was still placed by these families on other informal sources: almost half of those with pre-school children and three-quarters of those with older children.

Among the comparatively small group of *single earner* households in which only the mother was employed, husbands, predictably, figured even more prominently, with 75% involved in child care. However, only 39% of those with pre-school children were sole carers, and just half in families with children over five. This indicates the limited extent to which fathers in these 'role reversal' families had taken on the burden of family responsibilities.

The role of formal provision

Much has been written over the years of the inadequacy of extra-familial care provision in Britain, especially publicly-provided services, for the children of working parents (Ferri, 1992; Moss, 1990). A closer look at the formal care used by the NCDS mothers confirmed that this picture did not appear to have changed.

Overall, less than half (43%) of those with under-fives included formal provision in their arrangements, and for only 27% was this their

Table 9   **Child-care packages used by cohort mothers according to: age of youngest child, husband's employment situation and own working hours.**

	husband: working mother works:			husband: not working	all
	<16 hours	16 - 34 hrs	35 + hrs		
youngest child under 5:	%	%	%	%	%
husband only	37	15	4	39	21
husband + informal	13	13	4	18	10
husband + formal	2	5	3	4	4
husband + informal + formal	2	5	4	14	4
informal only	22	26	34	4	26
formal only	16	29	44	14	27
informal + formal	8	10	6	7	8
total	**100**	**100**	**100**	**100**	**100**
(n)	**(263)**	**(279)**	**(156)**	**(28)**	**(726)**
youngest child over 5:					
husband only	37	19	9	50	22
husband + informal	27	27	26	21	26
husband + formal	–	1	3	4	1
husband + informal + formal	1	2	1	–	1
informal only	34	45	41	12	40
formal only	1	5	14	–	6
informal + formal	1	2	6	12	3
total	**100**	**100**	**100**	**100**	**100**
(n)	**(116)**	**(269)**	**(140)**	**(24)**	**(549)**

sole source of child care (Table 9). Mothers who worked full-time (35 or more hours a week) were the group most likely to rely on formal services (57% altogether and 44% using only this). Looking at the *type* of formal provision showed that 33% of mothers of pre-school children had day care (of whom two-thirds relied solely on this), while just 11% used educational provision (which met the full needs of 2%) (Table 3.1).

Formal care provision was used by only 11% of cohort mothers whose youngest child was five or over, and was the sole source of care in just half these cases (Table 9). (It should be noted that statutory education, which all children aged five and over were assumed to attend, was omitted from the analysis.) Again, those working 35 hours a week or more were most likely to use formal care (24% in all, and 14% using only this). Not surprisingly, formal education provision other than statutory schooling was practically non-existent for this age group, but day-care services also met only a tiny proportion of the need: just 8% of mothers had formal day-care provision, and in only half of these cases was it the sole source of care (Table 3.1).

These findings highlight once more the lack of public provision for children of working parents, especially those of school age. When informal and paternal care are added together for the over-fives (from Table 9), we can see that this accounted for almost all of the care arrangements made by working mothers, regardless of their working hours. For the great majority, therefore, the immediate or extended family was a crucial source of support in balancing the demands of employment and parenting. From this it might be concluded that, in practice, the policy for child care to be the private responsibility of parents relates not only to the arranging, but also to the *providing*, of care.

Parenting roles in the home

From the findings reported so far, it is clear that fathers were an important source of child care in families with working mothers. But this does not tell us everything about the division of parenting and other work within the household, and how this related to each parent's employment position.

One of the self-completion questionnaires used for the NCDS5 survey presented cohort members with a list of domestic tasks and asked whether, in their family, each was done mainly by themselves, their partner, someone else, or shared more or less equally. As far as caring for and bringing up children were concerned, there were three relevant topics:

- *generally being with and looking after children*

- *looking after children when they are ill*

- *teaching children good behaviour.*

Overall, the responses showed that general care was almost invariably undertaken either mainly by the mother or shared equally by the couple. More than half (54%) of the mothers claimed it was mostly their responsibility and almost all of the remainder (45%) that it was shared (Table 3.2). Among the fathers, 48% reported that their wives did most of this work, and 50% said it was a joint responsibility. The dominant role of mothers was even more striking in relation to looking after sick children, with the proportion of cases in which the mother was said to be the main provider of such care rising to 65% among cohort fathers and 69% among cohort mothers (Table 3.3).

A very different picture emerged in relation to teaching children good behaviour, since here the great majority of both fathers (85%) and mothers (82%) claimed that this aspect of parenting was shared equally (Table 3.4). It is also, of course, a less time-bound activity than providing general or nursing care, and this picture of much greater paternal involvement is consistent with the traditional notion of the disciplinary role of the father. That it is also a particularly *male* perception is indicated by the fact that 4% of fathers, but just 1% of mothers, said that the father took the lead, as opposed to a shared, role in this; and the figures rose to 14% and 5% respectively among parents of adolescents. It is also interesting to note that on every measure of parental involvement, fathers claimed rather more participation in terms of joint or sole responsibility than mothers reported in relation to their husbands; a discrepancy which has also been noted in other studies (e.g. Bjornberg, 1992; Gershuny and Jones, 1987).

Our main interest, however, lay in how these parenting tasks were carried out in the different employment groups. In general, the findings showed that while fathers' involvement increased according to their wives' level of participation in the labour market, the balance of responsibility remained with mothers.

The most egalitarian domestic arrangements were found in the *dual earner families* in which both parents worked full-time. Here, *general child care* was most commonly reported to be a shared task – by two-thirds of cohort mothers and three-quarters of cohort fathers (Table 10). Where this did not happen, however, the traditional role division prevailed, with a quarter of the fathers and a third of the mothers claiming that child care was largely a maternal responsibility. These findings echo those of the Day Care Study carried out by the Thomas Coram Research Unit (Brannen and Moss, 1991). When mothers worked part-time only, the proportion of cases in which they themselves were mainly responsible for child care rose considerably: to more than half in the reports of the cohort mothers, and over 40% according to cohort fathers.

Similar differences between the full-time and part-time dual earners were found in relation to caring for sick children, albeit at the lower overall level of paternal involvement noted above (Table 11).These findings strongly indicate, therefore, that when both parents are employed, it is the mother, irrespective of whether she herself is working full-time or part-time, who takes time off to look after children when they are ill. This was also the situation

| Table 10 | 'Who is normally responsible for generally being with and looking after children': by parents' employment situation |

cohort fathers:	dual earner:		single earner:		no earner
	wife ft	wife pt	wife home	wife works	
	%	%	%	%	%
mostly father	2	1	<1	16	3
mostly wife	24	42	68	21	45
shared equally	72	57	32	61	53
someone else	2	–	<1	2	–
total	100	100	100	100	100
(n)	(397)	(993)	(1008)	(44)	(78)

cohort mothers:	dual earner:		single earner:		no earner
	mother ft	mother pt	mother home	mother works	
	%	%	%	%	%
mostly mother	32	52	72	26	45
mostly husband	1	<1	–	9	1
shared equally	66	48	28	64	54
someone else	1	–	–	1	–
total	100	100	100	100	100
(n)	(532)	(1261)	(953)	(66)	(83)

Table 11 'Who is normally responsible for looking after children when ill': by parents' employment situation

cohort fathers:	dual earner:		single earner:		no earner
	wife ft	wife pt	wife home	wife works	
	%	%	%	%	%
mostly father	2	1	<1	11	4
mostly wife	45	65	76	36	45
shared equally	52	34	23	50	51
someone else	1	–	–	2	–
total	**100**	**100**	**100**	**100**	**100**
(n)	**(396)**	**(992)**	**(1010)**	**(44)**	**(78)**

cohort mothers:	dual earner:		single earner:		no earner
	mother ft	mother pt	mother home	mother works	
	%	%	%	%	%
mostly mother	54	69	80	48	66
mostly husband	1	1	–	2	–
shared equally	44	30	20	50	34
someone else	1	–	–	–	–
total	**100**	**100**	**100**	**100**	**100**
(n)	**(531)**	**(1260)**	**(953)**	**(64)**	**(83)**

reported by Brannen and Moss (1991), although Kiernan (1992) found that fathers had increased their contribution in this area.

The *actual* situation reported by the cohort parents with regard to caring for sick children was compared with the beliefs they expressed about what *should* happen. They were asked to indicate their support for a number of statements, on a five-point scale ranging from 'strongly agree' to 'strongly disagree'. One of these was: *'if a child is ill and both parents are working, it should usually be the mother who takes time off to look after the child'.*

Parents who both worked full-time were less likely to agree with this statement than those in households where the mother worked part-time. In each of the dual earner groups, however, the number who said that it *should* be the mother who takes time off work was much smaller than the number who said that this actually happened (Tables 11 and 12). Interestingly, regardless of their employment situation, mothers were more

likely than fathers to agree that it *should* be the mother who takes time off work. One can only speculate as to how far this reflects their views of maternal and paternal roles in nursing children, or of the couples' respective job responsibilities. It has been observed elsewhere that the social construct of the 'good' mother includes giving priority to child care, especially for the very young, and that social expectations of women's care responsibilities are strongly endorsed by women themselves; while it has also been suggested that women may be reluctant to relinquish a role which is central to their self-identity as mothers (Brannen and Moss, 1988; Petersen, 1994; Lamb *et al.*, 1987).

The division of child care between parents in both full- and part-time dual earner families was also influenced by the number of hours they worked. Among the cohort *fathers* whose wives worked full-time, eight out of ten shared child care if they themselves worked less than 50 hours a week, but if they did longer hours, the proportion

Table 12 'If a child is ill and both parents are working, it should be the mother who takes time off to look after the child': by parents' employment situation

	cohort fathers: dual earner:		cohort mothers: dual earner:	
	wife ft	wife pt	mother ft	mother pt
	%	%	%	%
strongly agree	4	5	6	8
agree	17	38	34	40
uncertain	13	14	6	9
disagree	38	36	41	36
strongly disagree	17	7	14	6
total	**100**	**100**	**100**	**100**
(n)	**(406)**	**(1002)**	**(540)**	**(1263)**

dropped to around half (Figure 5 (b)). Similarly, two-thirds of fathers with part-time working wives played an equal part in the care of children if they themselves worked less than 50 hours; if they exceeded this, fewer than half did so.

Looking at the relationship between cohort *mothers'* working hours and general child care showed an apparently different pattern, since the proportion reporting that care was shared equally *rose* in line with hours worked, from 43% among those working under 16 hours a week to 70% in the group working more than 35 hours(Figure 5 (a)). What this means, of course, is that while, as *fathers'* hours increased, their working wives were increasingly likely to be *solely* responsible for child care, when *mothers* worked longer hours, the corresponding rise was in *shared* care. In virtually no case did major responsibility transfer to the father.

In the 'traditional' *single earner* family, involving a full-time working father and a home-based mother, maternal responsibility for general child care was, predictably, the norm (reported by 68% of fathers and 72% of mothers: Table 10). These fathers were less than half as likely to share child care as were those with full-time working wives. The significance of their own working hours for their participation in child care remained, however: just over a third of those working less than 50 hours said they shared it,

and the figure dropped to one in four among those working longer hours.

Among the small group in which the mother was the sole earner, the key question was: did home-based fathers take over the major responsibility for child care from their working wives? The responses showed that, far from this being the case, *shared* care was the most common arrangement, and where one parent assumed major responsibility, it was much more likely to be the mother, as indicated by 21% of the fathers and 26% of the mothers (Table 10). Although this was the only group in which a sizeable proportion of fathers were said to be the major care provider, this occurred only when the mother worked more than 35 hours a week (Figure 5 (b)). The picture was even more marked in relation to caring for sick children: according to the cohort mothers, just 2% of their non-employed husbands took on this role and 48% did it themselves (Table 11). This suggests that the mothers took time off work even when their husbands were at home, and that the notion of 'role reversal' implied by the employment position of parents in such families was hardly borne out in terms of the allocation of child-care responsibilities. In fact, the pattern of child care in these families was not very different from those with both parents working full-time. These findings are in line with those of other studies

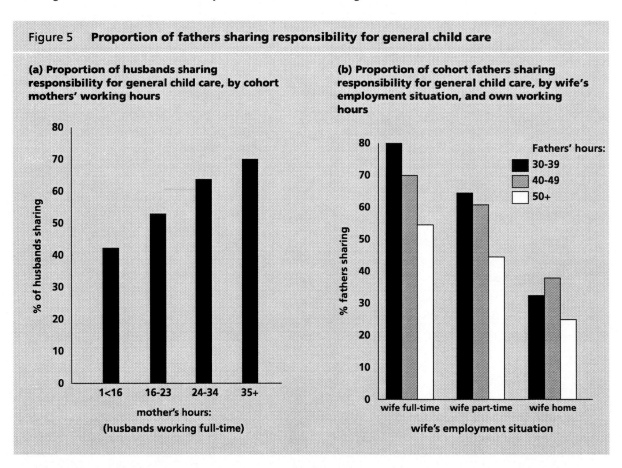

Figure 5   **Proportion of fathers sharing responsibility for general child care**

(a) Proportion of husbands sharing responsibility for general child care, by cohort mothers' working hours

(b) Proportion of cohort fathers sharing responsibility for general child care, by wife's employment situation, and own working hours

which have found the lowest level of domestic role-sharing in households with unemployed men and women in part-time employment (Wheelock, 1990).

In the *no earner* families, equal sharing of child care was less common than in the 'role reversal' households, so that the picture here did not echo the relatively egalitarian pattern in families with two full-time working parents. Just over half of both the mothers and fathers in no earner households reported that child care was equally shared between them, and in almost all of the remaining cases it was provided by the mother (Table 10). While these findings may reflect a reluctance among non-employed fathers to take on a greater domestic role, it may also be the case that the maternal resistence to 'shared' parenting referred to above is particularly strong among mothers who are not themselves in the labour force, and who regard the home and children as their own domain of responsibility and expertise.

Working unsocial hours

The relationship between working unsocial hours and child-care patterns within the home environment was a problematic area of analysis. Although details were available about the actual hours or days worked by the cohort members, we knew only whether their wives or husbands were working full-time or part-time. It was not possible, therefore, to gauge precisely how far unsocial hours represented 'shift parenting', with one partner working while the other was at home.

Although the differences which emerged from the analysis were small, they diverged for mothers and for fathers. Overall, cohort fathers who worked in the evening were slightly less likely to share in general child care than those who did not (49% versus 53%: Table 3.6). It is likely, of course, that evening work accounts for the long hours reported, either at the workplace or in bringing work home. The difference remained among fathers with working wives, but was not found among those with home-based wives, suggesting that the otherwise greater involvement of fathers whose partners were also employed was somewhat eroded when they themselves worked in the evenings. Similarly, fathers in dual full-time earner families were rather less likely to play an equal part in child care if they worked at the weekend (Table 3.7). There were no differences however, according to whether or not fathers worked at nights, either overall or when the couple's employment

situation was examined (Table 3.8). In other words, being around the home during the day, even if their wives were working, did not appear to increase fathers' level of involvement in child care.

By contrast, cohort mothers who worked any form of unsocial hours reported rather *more* shared child care than those who did not. This would seem to suggest that, as noted earlier, many mothers worked at times when their partners were available to care for the children. These differing trends for mothers and fathers add further support to the view that fathers' working conditions strongly influence their contribution to family life, while for mothers, it is their family circumstances which determine the nature of their labour market participaption.

Social and educational background

Popular conceptions suggest that the involved, family-oriented father is more likely to be found in middle-class households. Previous research in this area has, however, produced conflicting findings: some studies (e.g. O'Brien, 1982) found working-class fathers more participative, others (e.g. Lewis *et al.*, 1982) that middle-class fathers were more involved. Our findings revealed a marked *inverse* relationship between social class of occupation and the level of shared child care. Among fathers, just 40% of those in professional jobs played an equal part with their wives, compared with 58% among semi-skilled or unskilled workers (Table 13). The pattern among mothers was similar: on the basis of their *husbands'* social class of occupation (in order to permit comparison with the fathers' group), only 35% of those in the professional group, and 39% in the managerial, said that their husbands shared the care of children, compared with 52% of those in the semi- and unskilled categories.

Since there is a social class difference in the ages at which couples become parents, it was important to take account of the age structure of the families of this sample of 33-year-old parents. Among the cohort fathers, the difference remained when age of youngest child was taken into account, as it did among mothers with children under five (Table 3.9).

Arrangements for the care of sick children showed the same clear trend, with less involvement by fathers in higher social class occupations (Table 3.10). Interestingly, however, replies to the question concerning who *should* look after children when they are ill showed a difference in the opposite direction (Table 3.11).

Table 13 **'Who is normally responsible for generally being with and looking after children':**
by social class of occupation

Cohort fathers:		social class of occupation:				
	professional/ managerial	skilled non-manual	skilled manual	semi/ unskilled	all
	%	%	%	%	%	%
mostly father	1	1	2	1	1	1
mostly wife	58	54	45	46	41	49
shared equally	40	44	52	53	58	50
someone else	1	1	1	–	–	–
total	**100**	**100**	**100**	**100**	**100**	**100**
(n)	**(172)**	**(805)**	**(313)**	**(818)**	**(342)**	**(2503)**
cohort mothers:						
mostly mother	65	60	55	50	48	55
mostly husband	–	–	–	–	<1	<1
shared equally	35	39	44	49	52	45
someone else	<1	1	<1	–	–	<1
total	**100**	**100**	**100**	**100**	**100**	**100**
(n)	**(213)**	**(907)**	**(320)**	**(869)**	**(458)**	**(2767)**

It would seem, then, that middle-class parents tended to express more egalitarian attitudes, but that this was not reflected in their actual behaviour.

Since parents' working hours were related to how child care was managed within the home, and fathers in higher social class occupations worked longer hours, it seemed possible that this could explain their lower involvement in child care. However, looking at cohort fathers who worked fewer than 50 hours a week showed that there was still a marked social class difference in their parenting contribution. Just 49% of professional fathers shared in the general care of their children compared with 62% of those in semi- and unskilled occupations (Table 3.12). Among those who worked more than 50 hours, there was no consistent pattern, except that professional fathers still showed by far the lowest level of involvement (19% – about half that in all the other occupational groups).

It was also interesting to find that there was an inverse relationship between the cohort father's highest educational qualification and his involvement in child care. Thus, for example, while only 35% of graduate fathers said that they and their wives were equally responsible for child care, the figure for those with no qualifications was 59% (Table 14), a striking difference only partially explained by the higher social class, longer working hours and younger families of the highly qualified fathers. It did seem, therefore, that the most highly educated men, particularly graduates, played relatively little part in the care of their children. It is likely that these 33-year-old fathers were at a stage when their commitment to career development was at a peak, and

involvement in family life consequently lessened. However, we have also seen that higher qualifications and social class of occupation were characteristic of those in dual full-time earner households, in which *shared* parenting roles were most common. These apparently conflicting patterns would seem to point to particular tensions for such parents in reconciling the responsibilities of employment and family life (Lewis and Cooper, 1988).

Allocation of domestic roles

As well as asking about child-care arrangements, the NCDS5 survey obtained information on the cohort members' views and behaviour regarding domestic work. Two of the attitude statements on the self-completion questionnaire related to the division of general household labour:

• *men and women should do the same jobs around the house*

• *when both partners are working full-time the man should take an equal share of the domestic chores.*

Most respondents endorsed the first statement, but mothers showed a higher level of agreement than fathers. The more *equal* the couples' relationship to the labour market – i.e. dual earner families with both partners in full-time work, or no earner households with both at home – the higher the level of agreement (Table 3.13). The lowest level of agreement was in 'traditional' single worker households where father/husband worked full-time and the wife/mother was at home.

There was overwhelming support from all

Parenting in the 1990s

| Table 14 | 'Who is normally responsible for generally being with and looking after children': by parents' educational level |

cohort fathers:

	Highest qualification:						
cohort fathers:	none	some	O level	A level	other higher	degree	all
	%	%	%	%	%	%	%
mostly father	1	1	1	1	–	1	1
mostly wife	40	42	47	51	52	63	49
shared equally	59	56	51	48	47	35	49
someone else	–	1	–	–	1	1	1
total	100	100	100	100	100	100	100
(n)	(252)	(400)	(673)	(549)	(362)	(331)	(2657)

	Highest qualification:						
cohort mothers:	none	some	O level	A level	other higher	degree	all
	%	%	%	%	%	%	%
mostly mother	45	53	54	61	52	61	54
mostly husband	1	1	1	1	–	1	1
shared equally	54	46	45	38	48	37	45
someone else	–	–	–	–	1	1	<1
total	100	100	100	100	100	100	100
(n)	(343)	(599)	(1103)	(240)	(435)	(293)	(3013)

groups for the view that domestic chores should be equally shared when both partners were in full-time employment, although up to 10% of fathers expressed uncertainty or disagreement, even when their wives were working full-time (Table 3.14).

The survey also collected information on who was, in practice, mainly responsible for a number of domestic tasks, including:

- *doing the shopping*

- *cleaning the home*

- *laundry and ironing*

- *household repairs, DIY, decorating*

- *looking after household money and paying bills.*

Recent studies have noted a trend for households with two full-time earners to reconcile the demands of employment and family life by purchasing domestic and child-care services (e.g. Gregson and Lowe, 1993; Pahl, 1984). Our findings indicated, however, that this solution was adopted by only a small minority of these families (around 7%) in relation to household cleaning and laundry. The replies showed that, while the highest levels of shared responsibility occurred in families with both parents in full-time employment, the most common situation was for mothers to be carrying the main burden (Tables 3.15–3.20). Thus, for example, two-thirds of full-time working mothers said they were responsible for cooking and cleaning, and four out of five for laundry. This continuing inequality in the division

of housework, even when women work full-time, has also been observed in other studies (Brannen, 1994; Martin and Roberts, 1984; Warde and Hetherington, 1993).

It was also striking that, in relation to housework, dual earner families in which the mother worked *part-time* differed very little from single earner households in which the mother was at home, thus reinforcing the view that these mothers 'fit' their employment roles around the domestic tasks for which they are predominantly responsible. There was little father involvement in housework in families in which they were the sole earners, except in relation to shopping, which just one in four fathers and mothers reported as a shared task.

The reports of cohort mothers with unemployed husbands showed little evidence of a greater paternal contribution, even when the mother herself was working. In fact, two-thirds of these working mothers said that they themselves were mainly responsible for cooking, cleaning and shopping, and four-fifths for washing and ironing. In contrast, cohort fathers who were out of the labour force, and whose wives were employed, were much more likely than any other group to claim that *they* bore the brunt of these chores.

The only domestic tasks which were undertaken mostly by fathers (about three-quarters in each group) were, predictably, household repairs and DIY, with little variation according to the couple's employment situation. Finally, the management of household finances showed much greater variation than any other domestic activity. In general, however, mothers were more likely than fathers to take major responsibility, especially in no earner families; a further indication, perhaps, of the emasculated role of unemployed fathers. The only exception was among single earner cohort fathers, who were more likely to see themselves as the main money-handlers. Interestingly, this was not the picture presented by home-based cohort mothers with working husbands.

Child-care patterns in the cohort members' families of origin

Having seen the great variation in paternal involvement with children among the 33-year-old fathers, we now turn to the data from earlier NCDS surveys to see whether there was any link between this and the pattern in their own families of origin. While empirical evidence in this field is sparse, two very different theoretical perspectives have been advanced: the first proposing that everyone internalises the model of parenting presented in their own families of upbringing; the other that many people consciously reject this model and adopt opposing approaches themselves (Belsky, 1984).

At both the seven-year (NCDS1) and eleven-year (NCDS2) follow-ups, the interview with the cohort member's parent (almost always the mother) asked for information about the part played by the father in 'managing the child'. The three main response categories included:

• *father takes a big/equal part with mother*

• *father takes a smaller but significant part*

• *father takes a very small part/leaves to mother.*

The term 'managing the child' clearly does not equate precisely with those employed in the NCDS5 survey; it could be said to fall somewhere in between *'generally looking after children'* and *'teaching children good behaviour'*. We therefore looked at both of these measures, according to the reported involvement of the cohort members' *own* fathers, to see whether there was any relationship between their current patterns of child care and what they themselves had experienced in their family of upbringing.

The seven-year data showed no relationship at all regarding general child care or teaching children good behaviour. For example, half of the cohort fathers whose *own* fathers had been highly involved left child care largely to their wives, as did those who had had less participative fathers (Table 15). Similarly, almost half of those whose fathers had played little part now shared equally in the care of their own children. As far as teaching good behaviour was concerned, the same high level of joint responsibility for this was reported regardless of the paternal role in the family of origin (Table 16). The same picture emerged when the 11-year data were examined. This might be interpreted as indicating little inter-generational link in parenting behaviour; alternatively, it is possible that contrasting trends to repeat or reject childhood experiences cancelled one another out.

It is also worth commenting in these analyses on the overall level of paternal involvement recorded during the childhood years of the cohort. While bearing in mind that the measures are not exactly equivalent, and may have held rather different meanings in the 1960s and 1990s, it is none the less striking that, in 1965, six out of ten fathers of the cohort were described as

Table 15 **'Who is normally responsible for generally being with and looking after children': by cohort member's *own* father's involvement in managing children at age 7 (NCDS1)**

cohort fathers:	**cohort members' father's part in managing child at age 7:**		
	equal to mother	**< mother but significant**	**small part/ leaves to mother**
	%	**%**	**%**
mostly father	1	1	2
mostly wife	49	48	51
shared equally	50	51	47
total	**100**	**100**	**100**
(n)	**(1392) (62%)**	**(669) (30%)**	**(181) (8%)**
cohort mothers:			
mostly mother	55	52	52
mostly husband	<1	1	–
shared equally	45	47	48
total	**100**	**100**	**100**
(n)	**(1588) (60%)**	**(782) (30%)**	**(263) (10%)**

Parenting in the 1990s

Table 16 **'Who is normally responsible for teaching children good behaviour': by cohort member's *own* father's involvement in managing children at age 7 (NCDS1)**

cohort fathers:	cohort members' father's part in managing child at age 7:		
	equal to mother	< mother but significant	small part/ leaves to mother
	%	%	%
mostly father	4	3	3
mostly wife	11	12	12
shared equally	85	85	85
total	**100**	**100**	**100**
(n)	**(1388) (62%)**	**(673) (30%)**	**(181) (8%)**
cohort mothers:			
mostly mother	16	18	18
mostly husband	1	1	1
shared equally	83	81	81
total	**100**	**100**	**100**
(n)	**(1597) (60%)**	**(782) (30%)**	**(262) (10%)**

playing an equal part in managing their children. This is higher than the figures for general child care relating to the cohort fathers themselves, although lower than those relating to teaching children good behaviour. O'Brien (1992), reviewing the relatively few studies in Britain and the United States which have investigated change in paternal participation over time, concluded that any evidence of increased father involvement with children was slight and inconsistent. Our own findings thus emphasise the need for caution regarding any claim that there has been a radical shift in the parenting role of fathers over the past generation.

4 Family cohesiveness and parenting behaviour

The last chapter described the diverse situations in which the NCDS parents were raising their children, in terms of the couples' employment status and working hours, and how these related to their parenting roles in child care and domestic work. Now we explore further the links between employment and family life. Did the parents' relationship to the labour market, in particular the amount of time this made available for home life, have any bearing on family functioning and parenting behaviour?

The first aspect of the home environment which was of interest here was family 'cohesiveness', indicated by the extent to which all family members were involved in joint activities. Current discourse in this area is replete with largely anecdotal or impressionistic claims about the erosion of 'family life', in terms of reduced frequency of joint meals and other activities, and of contact with wider kin networks. The dual earner family is the particular focus of such perceptions; as a recent Danish report commented: 'we are all aware that these families spend too little time together' (Carlsen and Larsen, 1994). Robust empirical evidence remains somewhat sparse, although recent studies have begun to establish links between family cohesiveness and the self-esteem of children and adolescents (e.g. Sweeting and West, 1995). The NCDS survey information about a range of family-based activities was, therefore, important in enabling us to investigate whether, for example, families in which both parents worked full-time, or where one or both worked long or unsocial hours, spent less time together in the ways referred to. We were also able to investigate whether children's own social lives were affected by their parents' employment situation.

The findings showed that having both parents employed full-time did not, of itself, mean less family cohesiveness. Whether mothers worked or not, or for how many hours, made little difference to the frequency of family activities. Fathers' working hours, on the other hand, *did* make a difference, with joint activities less common among those who worked long hours.

Another topic of interest was parents' actual behaviour in relation to their children. Again, relatively little is known about how children are being brought up in the many different social and economic circumstances which form the context for parenting today, and the NCDS survey provided a wealth of information on this. The overall picture obtained was thus of interest in itself, although here, too, our main focus was on whether parenting behaviour differed according to whether, and in what way, mothers and fathers were involved in the labour force. For example, was the varying amount of time available for family life linked to mothers' and fathers' interaction with their children, and to the role that children themselves were expected to play in the home environment?

The findings here revealed that older (10+) children with both parents working full-time were expected to be more responsible for self-care, especially if their mothers worked long hours. Other measures of parenting behaviour showed only small differences: mothers who worked full-time read rather less often to their young children than home-based mothers. On the other hand, fathers in dual full-time earner households were slightly *more* frequently involved in outdoor play with their children than their counterparts who were sole earners, although, again, such activity was reduced among fathers who worked long hours. The analysis of family cohesiveness and parenting behaviour also showed that fathers who shared the responsibility for the care and socialisation of their children were more likely to take part in activities involving the whole family and outdoor play with their children. These relationships contribute to a picture of more 'family-oriented' fathers, in the sense of showing more active participation in family life (Bjornberg, 1995).

Family activities

Questions on joint family activities were put to cohort mothers, or the wives of cohort fathers, who were part of a one-in-three sub-sample of the cohort who took part in the Mother and Child study. They were asked to indicate how often they were involved as a family (i.e. both parents and all children) in:

- *eating together*
- *spending an evening together*
- *shopping*
- *going out to eat, to the cinema/theatre, sports event or religious service*
- *visiting relatives/friends*
- *going on holiday.*

It would seem likely that family involvement in some of these activities would be particularly influenced by the time available for its members to be together, in others more by economic circumstances. As we have already seen, the employment situation of parent couples was of key importance to both family time and material resources, and this was, therefore, a major focus of analysis.

Parents' employment situation

There was nothing to indicate from the replies to these questions that *dual earner* families experienced less joint involvement in the activities listed than the 'traditional' *single earner* households in which only the father was employed. Nor were there any differences in the pattern of family activities *within* the dual earner group according to whether the mother worked full- or part-time. Dual earner families in fact appeared to shop together, go out (to the cinema, etc.), and to visit relatives and friends slightly *more* often than those in which only the father was working (Table 17). Overall, more than half of the respondents indicated that they saw relatives or friends at least once a week, and 90% that this happened once a month or more, a finding which challenges the notion of weakened social networks in families with two full-time earners (Brannen and Moss, 1991).

Similar proportions of dual and single (male) earner families ate together at least once a day. What is, perhaps, worth commenting on here is that, overall, as many as one in three mothers said that they did *not* do so! The great majority (over 90%) in each group spent at least one evening a week together, and there was also no difference in the frequency of family holidays: over 80% had at least one holiday a year, and one family in three enjoyed more than this.

The small group of families in which the *mother* was the single earner differed little from those in which only the father was employed, except that they were rather more likely to have a family meal at least once a day. They were less likely, however, to have frequent family outings – no doubt reflecting their relatively disadvantaged economic circumstances – although their experience of family holidays was similar.

The most striking differences were found between the *no earner* families and the other groups, particularly concerning those activities requiring financial resources. Families with no parent in the labour force contained by far the highest proportion who rarely or never went out together to the cinema, or for a meal (one in three, compared with one in ten among the dual earner families), who rarely or never had a family holiday (37% as against one in ten in all other groups) or who seldom shopped together. Paradoxically, they also showed the highest proportion who *frequently* went shopping as a family, probably indicating the greater amount of time, as opposed to financial resources, available in these households. Not surprisingly, perhaps, they also ate together more often than any other group. These findings provide a glimpse of the impact upon all family members of the material disadvantage resulting from parental disconnection from the labour market (see Dobson *et al.*, 1994).

Working hours and family activities

Although having both parents in employment made little difference to the pattern of joint activities, the hours worked by fathers *did* have an impact on this aspect of family life. We saw in Chapter 3 that fathers who worked long hours contributed less to child care and domestic work. This pattern was repeated in relation to family activities: for example, while over two-thirds of the cohort fathers who worked less than 40 hours a week had a family meal at least once a day, fewer than half of those working more than 50 hours did so (Table 4.1). One in five families with a father who worked long (50+) hours rarely or never went on family shopping expeditions, compared with fewer than one in ten in which he worked under 40 hours. Similarly, those with fathers working long hours made fewer family visits to friends or relatives.

Working unsocial hours made a much smaller difference, although families in which cohort fathers regularly worked in the evenings were less likely to share a family meal at least once a

Table 17   **Frequency of family activities by parents' employment status**

	dual earner:		single earner:		no earner	all
	mother ft	**mother pt**	**mother home**	**mother works**		
a) eating together	%	%	%	%	%	%
once a day or more	61	61	64	76	81	63
several times/week	22	26	19	14	8	22
once a week or less	12	11	15	10	7	12
never/hardly ever	4	1	2	—	3	2
varies	1	1	1	—	—	1
total	**100**	**100**	**100**	**100**	**100**	**100**
(n)	**(319)**	**(706)**	**(634)**	**(42)**	**(59)**	**(1760)**
b) spending an evening together						
once a week or more	91	95	94	95	97	94
less often	4	3	2	2	—	3
never/hardly ever	2	1	2	2	2	2
varies	3	1	2	—	2	2
total	**100**	**100**	**100**	**100**	**100**	**100**
(n)	**(308)**	**(692)**	**(610)**	**(42)**	**(59)**	**(1711)**
c) shopping together						
once a week or more	49	44	40	42	53	44
once a month or more	27	29	34	33	29	30
less often	5	8	7	12	3	7
never/hardly ever	17	17	17	7	22	17
varies	2	2	2	7	3	2
total	**100**	**100**	**100**	**100**	**100**	**100**
(n)	**(315)**	**(707)**	**(629)**	**(42)**	**(59)**	**(1753)**
d) going out to eat, cinema, etc.)						
once a week or more	26	24	27	23	19	25
once a month or more	46	46	42	33	23	44
less often	16	14	13	26	21	15
never/hardly ever	9	13	17	14	32	14
varies	2	3	2	5	5	2
total	**100**	**100**	**100**	**100**	**100**	**100**
(n)	**(304)**	**(684)**	**(589)**	**(43)**	**(57)**	**(1677)**
e) visiting relatives/ friends						
once a week or more	53	52	47	49	54	51
once a month or more	37	37	41	33	29	38
less often	8	6	9	12	10	7
never/hardly ever	2	4	2	5	3	2
varies	1	2	1	2	3	1
total	**100**	**100**	**100**	**100**	**100**	**100**
(n)	**(316)**	**(705)**	**(641)**	**(43)**	**(59)**	**(1764)**
f) family holiday						
more than once a year	53	52	47	49	54	51
once a year	37	37	41	33	29	38
every 2/3 years	8	6	9	12	10	7
never/hardly ever	2	4	2	5	3	2
varies	1	2	1	2	3	1
total	**100**	**100**	**100**	**100**	**100**	**100**
(n)	**(316)**	**(705)**	**(641)**	**(43)**	**(59)**	**(1764)**

day (55% compared with 70% of other families), and also visited relatives and friends less frequently (Table 4.2). There was a similar, though much weaker, trend among families of cohort fathers who worked at night, but no relationship at all between weekend working and the level of family activities.

In contrast to fathers, the total hours worked by mothers showed no association with the frequency of family activities (Table 4.3). Similarly, there was very little variation according to whether mothers worked unsocial hours (Table 4.4).

Social background

It also appeared that the typical experiences of family activity varied between the social class groups; those from manual backgrounds were characterised by home-based contact and extended family and social networks, and the non-manual groups more oriented towards consumer activities outside the home environment. Families with fathers in manual occupations ate together more frequently: three-quarters of those in semi- or unskilled groups did so at least once a day, compared with just over half in the professional/ managerial class (Table 4.5). They also visited their relatives and friends more often. It seems likely that the direction of these differences reflected, at least to some extent, the longer hours worked by fathers in professional and managerial occupations. Families with fathers in non-manual occupations, on the other hand, reported more frequent family outings and holidays, which was no doubt linked to their more favourable economic circumstances.

Fathers' involvement with children

We saw in Chapter 3 that there was considerable variation in the extent to which fathers were involved with their children, as measured by how parents shared the tasks of child care and socialisation. To examine whether this was related to family cohesiveness in terms of joint activities, father involvement was categorised into four levels, according to whether he took equal responsibility with the mother for:

- *both child care and teaching good behaviour (high involvement)*

- *child care only*

- *teaching behaviour only*

- *neither (low involvement).*

Families with 'highly involved' fathers showed more cohesiveness in terms of joint activities: they ate together, shopped together, went on family outings, and visited relatives and friends more frequently than those in which fathers were relatively uninvolved with their children (Table 18). The links between these two sets of measures would seem to point to a group of relatively 'family-oriented' fathers, who shared with mothers the responsibility for the care and upbringing of their children, and who also participated in a range of activities involving all members of the family.

Children's social activities

We were also able to examine whether parents' employment patterns had any bearing on their children's own social lives, as well as on activities involving the whole family. Mothers were asked how often their children's friends came to the

Table 18   Family activities by level of paternal involvement with children

a) eating together	father's involvement: high %	low %		d) going out (to eat, to cinema etc.)	high %	low %
once a day or more	71	56		once a week or more	26	24
several times/week	20	27		once a month or more	45	44
once a week or less	6	14		less often	13	16
never/hardly	2	3		never/hardly	12	15
varies	1	1		varies	3	2
total	100	100		total	100	100
(n)	(420)	(188)		(n)	(408)	(178)

b) spending an evening together	high %	low %		e) visiting relatives/friends	high %	low %
once a week or more	94	91		once a week or more	57	41
less often	2	5		once a month or more	33	43
never/hardly	2	2		less often	7	11
varies	1	2		never/hardly	2	3
				varies	1	2
total	100	100		total	100	100
(n)	(420)	(188)		(n)	(421)	(189)

c) shopping together	high %	low %		f) family holiday	high %	low %
once a week or more	53	38		more than once a year	33	35
once a month or more	26	29		once a year	48	44
less often	5	11		every 2/3 years	8	4
never/hardly	13	21		never/hardly	10	14
varies	3	2		varies	1	3
total	100	100		total	100	100
(n)	(422)	(189)		(n)	(418)	(187)

home – to play, have tea and so on. Overall, more than seven out of ten said this happened once a week or more, but it was slightly less frequent in families in which the mother worked full-time, and especially where she was the sole earner (Table 19). Having a mother who worked long (35+) hours was particularly associated with less frequent visits from other children; one child in ten in this group rarely or never had friends in their home (Table 4.6). The hours worked by fathers, on the other hand, was not related in any way, nor was their overall level of involvement in child care. This indicates that it is essentially mothers who bear the responsibility for organising and facilitating children's social lives, and that this is likely to be made more difficult by heavy demands of work outside the home.

Parenting behaviour

The mothers interviewed for the survey were also asked for information about specific aspects of parenting behaviour in relation to each child in the family in different age groups: under three years, three to five, six to nine, and ten and over. This included questions about direct parent–child *interaction*, including:

- *how often mothers read to their children, and*

- *the amount of time fathers spent with them in outdoor activities.*

Another area of enquiry concerned the frequency and methods of *disciplining* children aged six and over, and also of showing *praise and approval.* Mothers were asked how many times in the previous week they had:

- *smacked their child*

- *kept him/her indoors*

- *taken away TV or other privileges*

- *taken away pocket money*

- *sent the child to his/her room*

and, similarly, how often they had:

- *shown the child physical affection*

- *praised the child for doing something worthwhile*

- *told another adult something positive about the child.*

Summary scores were calculated for these two areas, based on the number of individual actions which had been adopted at least once. This produced a maximum score of 5 for 'punishments', and of 3 for 'praise'.

A note of caution is needed here concerning these measures and their interpretation. Clearly, they do not cover the whole spectrum of parenting behaviour, nor can any conclusions be drawn here regarding any impact on children's well-being and development (although the importance of praise and affection is hardly in doubt). Also, we would explicitly reject an assumption of gendered parental roles implicit in the way the questions were framed.

In addition to the direct parenting behaviour of the mothers and fathers, a further set of questions related to their expectations of their children's contribution to domestic tasks, in terms of self-care. Mothers of children aged six and upwards were asked how often the children concerned were expected to:

- *make their own bed*

- *clean their own room*

- *clean up after spills*

- *bath or wash themselves*

- *clear or tidy up after themselves.*

Here too, a summary score was derived with three categories, ranging from 'low' expectations (less than half the time) to 'high' (more than half the time).

The mothers' replies were examined

	dual earner:		single earner:		no	all
	mother ft	mother pt	mother home	mother works	earner	
	%	%	%	%	%	%
once a week or more	68	73	71	60	79	71
once a month or more	19	21	23	29	18	22
never/hardly ever	10	4	5	12	2	6
varies	3	1	1	-	2	1
total	100	100	100	100	100	100
(n)	(284)	(681)	(590)	(42)	(57)	(1654)

Table 19 **How often children have friends to visit, by parents' employment situation**

separately for each age group concerned. Thus, parents with more than one child were likely to be represented in more than one group. However, it is also the case that parental behaviour may vary in relation to children of different ages. Also, since this information was obtained from only the one-in-three sub-sample, there were few examples from among the no earner families or those in which the mother was the single earner. The analysis therefore compares dual earner families, with the mother working full- or part-time, and those in which only the father was employed.

Parents' employment situation

The main differences to emerge in relation to parenting behaviour lay in what was expected of children. For those in the older age group (ten and over), a greater contribution was sought by parents in dual earner families, especially when both worked full-time: 31% in this group had a 'high' score, compared with 20% among part-time working mothers and just 13% among those not in work (Figure 6). This trend was particularly marked when the mothers worked long hours: 45% of those doing 35+ hours a week expected a 'high' contribution from their children, compared with only 8% of those working fewer than 16 hours (Figure 7).

In contrast to the mothers' working situation, the hours worked by fathers made no difference (Table 4.7). As we saw earlier, mothers bore the brunt of domestic work, regardless of the couples' employment situations, which would seem to explain why mothers', rather than fathers', working hours were related to what was expected of children. Although it should be stressed that the questions related to children's care of themselves and their own environment rather than housework generally, it is interesting to note that there were no differences in parents' expectations of boys and girls. It might be speculated, therefore, whether the daughters and sons of the NCDS cohort will, in due course, adopt more egalitarian domestic roles than their parents.

There were less-marked differences according to employment situation in relation to mothers' direct parenting behaviour towards children, in terms of reading to them and the use of discipline or praise. Overall, the great majority of all mothers with children aged three to five read to them at least three times a week. However, those who were employed full-time did so rather less often than those in other situations: 27% read just once a week or less compared with 13% among part-time workers and 16% of home-based

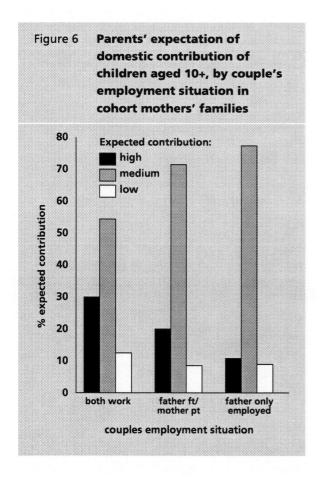

Figure 6   **Parents' expectation of domestic contribution of children aged 10+, by couple's employment situation in cohort mothers' families**

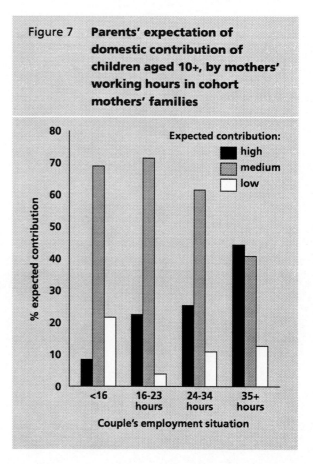

Figure 7   **Parents' expectation of domestic contribution of children aged 10+, by mothers' working hours in cohort mothers' families**

mothers (Figure 8). These figures probably underestimate the association with employment status, since, as we saw earlier, mothers working full-time tended to have higher educational qualifications and social class backgrounds, both of which were associated with *more* frequent reading to children. There is some evidence that being read to daily at a very young age is linked to higher reading scores in early adulthood (Bynner and Steedman, 1995). Such experiences may therefore be an important part of whatever substitute day-care arrangements are made for children of full-time working parents.

There was little variation in how much mothers disciplined or praised their children. For both the age groups concerned (under and over 10), mothers in dual full-time earner families recorded slightly less use of disciplinary behaviour than those who worked part-time, or were not in the labour force (Table 4.8), and, for older children, they also appeared to show slightly less praise or affection (Table 4.9). The obvious explanation for this would seem to lie in the relative amount of time spent together by mothers and children in the different groups.

The specific question put to mothers concerning fathers' behaviour focused on their involvement in outdoor activities with the children, reinforcing somewhat the stereotypical view of the paternal role. Overall, the majority of

fathers were reported as engaging in such activities at least once a week; predictably, perhaps, slightly more frequently with their sons than with their daughters. Just as fathers in dual full-time earner families had been more involved in the general care of their children, so they also spent more time in outdoor activities with them. This was most marked in relation to older (10+) children, 24% of fathers in this group doing so at least once a day, compared with only 14% of fathers with home-based wives (Figure 9). However, as had been the case with their contribution to child care, fathers' involvement in outdoor play was also related to their own working hours: daily activity of this kind was twice as common among those working under 50 hours a week as among fathers who spent longer at work (Table 4.10).

Social class

As with family activities, there were some variations according to fathers' social class of occupation in the ways in which parents behaved towards their children. For mothers, there was a marked difference in the frequency with which they read to their children, especially those aged three to five: six out of ten mothers from non-manual backgrounds read every day, compared with just four out of 10 of those with husbands in manual jobs (Table 4.11). There was no consistent

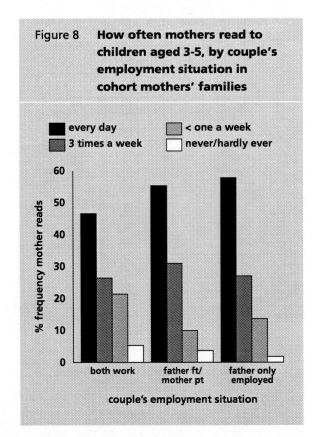

Figure 8 **How often mothers read to children aged 3-5, by couple's employment situation in cohort mothers' families**

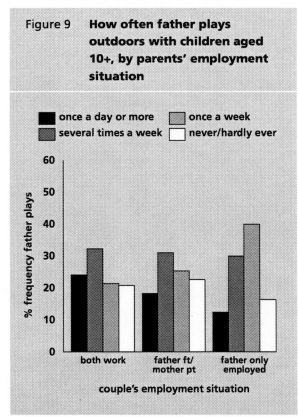

Figure 9 **How often father plays outdoors with children aged 10+, by parents' employment situation**

trend in the use of discipline, but, although only a small minority had used multiple methods (three or more), mothers from professional/managerial groups were least likely to have done so, especially in relation to older childen (Table 4.12). Also, mothers in the semi- and unskilled manual groups showed less praise/affection to older (10+) children: 19% had shown none at all, or only one form, in the past week, compared with just 4% of mothers from professional/managerial backgrounds (Table 4.13).

Fathers' involvement

While there were no consistent social background differences in parents' expectations of what their children should contribute to domestic work, fathers' level of involvement in child care *was* related to this. Rather more was expected of those with highly involved fathers than from those whose fathers took little part in either child care or socialisation. For children aged 10 and over, 31% and 11% respectively recorded 'high' expectations (Figure 10). The highly involved fathers were, of course, most likely to be found in the dual full-time earner families, in which they themselves also played a relatively large part in household tasks. These findings together point to an 'egalitarian' family ethos in which all members, parents and children alike, contribute to domestic work. Some would regard this in a positive light as encouraging responsibility and independence in children; others might view it more negatively as a burdensome encroachment on the freedom of childhood.

Fathers who were highly involved in child care were also the group who most frequently played outdoors with their children. However, those who did so *least* often were not the uninvolved, but the fathers whose role appeared to be largely concerned with teaching good behaviour (Table 4.14). This suggests that, for this group of fathers, their relationship with their children was based on a 'traditional' authoritarian paternal role. As far as the uninvolved fathers were concerned, the fact that they engaged in play with their children no less often than those who shared care responsibilities is in line with other studies which have found that paternal participation tends to focus on leisure pursuits, leaving the routine tasks such as washing and feeding in the mother's domain (Lamb, 1986; Martin and Roberts, 1984).

Fathers' overall level of involvement with the care and socialisation of their children also seemed to have some bearing on mothers' parenting behaviour. Mothers whose husbands were uninvolved read more often to their children than those with highly participative partners (62% versus 48% among mothers of three-to-five-year-olds: Table 4.15). This would seem to be a further indicator of the disproportionate amount of parenting responsibility undertaken by mothers in families in which the father's domestic role appears peripheral.

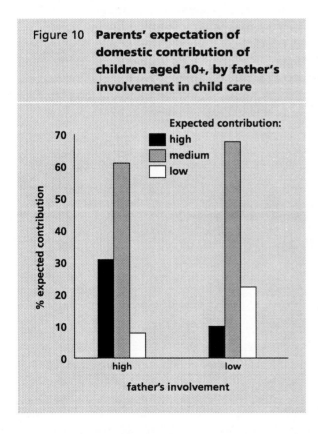

Figure 10 **Parents' expectation of domestic contribution of children aged 10+, by father's involvement in child care**

5 Parent outcomes

Our final area of investigation is concerned with the parents' feelings about their family situation, and their own well-being. More specifically, it focuses on their views about their marital relationships, their satisfaction with their lives to date, and assessments of their own mental health. Our particular interest, of course, was in whether the couples' employment circumstances were related in any way to these measures, and also whether the ways in which their respective parenting roles were undertaken had any bearing on such outcomes.

There has been some indication from previous research that women's marital happiness is linked to their family workload and their husbands' involvement with home and children (Lamb *et al.*, 1987), although not always in a consistent way. Belsky (1984), in a detailed review of research on parenting, points to the importance of sharing and equality in parenting roles, and the mutual support this entails, not only for parent's own well-being, but also for their adoption of parenting behaviour conducive to positive child development. Most research to date, however, has focused on *maternal* outcomes; there has been very little investigation of how various patterns of family life impinge on *paternal* perceptions and the emotive aspects of fatherhood.

In summarising the main findings in this area, it is important to note first that the great majority of both mothers and fathers appeared to be happy in their marriages and generally satisfied with their lives. Those in the 'traditional' single earner families, with only the father in employment, were the most positive in their responses, although only slightly more so than parents in dual earner households. More generally negative feelings were expressed by both mothers and fathers in no earner families and those in which the mother was the only parent in employment. Exclusion from the labour market was also strongly linked to symptoms of malaise among fathers, and among mothers with unemployed husbands, except when the mothers themselves were in paid work.

Parents' perceptions were also influenced by the degree of gender segregation in domestic roles. The extent to which fathers shared in the care and socialisation of their children was a key factor in mothers' satisfaction with their marital relationships and their lives in general. A substantial minority of those who bore the full weight of domestic responsibility themselves were unhappy with their situation, and for mothers in employment this discontent increased with the number of hours they spent in paid work. Mothers with uninvolved husbands were also more vulnerable to emotional disorder.

By contrast, fathers' marital happiness, overall life satisfaction and emotional state were only tenuously linked to their level of involvement with their children. In fact, high involvement showed a slight *negative* relationship to these outcomes, especially for fathers devoting long hours to their work outside the home. These findings for fathers and mothers together point to the stress produced by responding to heavy demands in both employment and family life.

Marital relationship

One of the items on the self-completion questionnaire asked those who were married or living as a couple: *'How happy is your relationship?'*. The responses were indicated on a scale ranging from 1 (extremely unhappy) to 7 (extremely happy). In an earlier project (Ferri and Smith, forthcoming (b)), we had classified those giving a rating of 4 or less as unhappy, since this correlated with other indicators of difficulty in the relationship. The same categorisation was used for the present study.

Further insight into the parents' marital relationships was provided by their indication of how much they and their partner agreed or disagreed about a number of topics, two of which were of particular interest here:

• *deciding how children should be brought up*

and

• *sharing household tasks*.

In the current climate of pessimism over the

state of marriage, perhaps the first point to note is that the great majority of the parents expressed positive feelings about their relationships: 80% of both fathers and mothers gave a rating of 6 or 7 (Table 5.1). (Interestingly, this was a similar level of response to that found among cohabiting mothers in McRae's (1993(b) study.) Slightly more mothers than fathers in the NCDS cohort indicated that they were less than happy (11% and 8% respectively).

Overall, about half of both fathers and mothers said they nearly always agreed on child-rearing, and just 4% in each case often or nearly always disagreed (Table 5.2).The range of responses regarding domestic work was much wider. Less than a quarter of both fathers and mothers said

they nearly always agreed on sharing household tasks, while 11% and 13% respectively often or nearly always disagreed (Table 5.3).

Marital happiness varied somewhat according to the couples' employment situation. The most contented groups appeared to be mothers and fathers in the 'traditional' *single earner* families in which only the father was in employment. The difference between them and the couples in *dual earner* households was not very large, however, and there was little variation *within* the latter group according to whether mothers worked full- or part-time (Table 20). Parents in families with only the father in employment also showed a slightly higher degree of consensus over child-rearing (Table 21),

Table 20   Cohort member's rating of relationship with spouse, by couple's employment situation

cohort fathers:		dual earner:		single earner:		no
		wife ft	wife pt	wife home	wife works	earner
		%	%	%	%	%
unhappy	(1-4)	10	8	6	21	15
	5	11	11	10	13	9
	6	32	8	33	32	22
happy	7	47	44	51	34	54
total		**100**	**100**	**100**	**100**	**100**
(n)		**(358)**	**(893)**	**(857)**	**(38)**	**(68)**

cohort mothers:		dual earner:		single earner:		no
		wife ft	wife pt	wife home	wife works	earner
		%	%	%	%	%
unhappy	(1-4)	15	10	22	9	23
	5	9	9	15	7	10
	6	33	35	22	32	26
happy	7	44	45	41	52	41
total		**100**	**100**	**100**	**100**	**100**
(n)		**(463)**	**(1117)**	**(54)**	**(847)**	**(69)**

Table 21   Consensus with partner about how children should be brought up, by couple's employment situation

cohort fathers:		dual earner:		single earner:		no
		wife ft	wife pt	wife home	wife works	earner
		%	%	%	%	%
always agree		47	52	55	45	49
often agree		35	30	30	39	24
sometimes agree		13	15	12	9	19
often/always agree		4	3	3	2	8
never talk about		<1	<1	–	5	–
total		**100**	**100**	**100**	**100**	**100**
(n)		**(400)**	**(994)**	**(1010)**	**(44)**	**(78)**

cohort mothers:		dual earner:		single earner:		no
		wife ft	wife pt	wife home	wife works	earner
		%	%	%	%	%
always agree		46	48	54	37	43
often agree		31	29	26	26	35
sometimes agree		18	24	16	31	15
often/always agree		4	1	3	6	7
never talk about		<1	<1	<1	–	–
total		**100**	**100**	**100**	**100**	**100**
(n)		**(538)**	**(1257)**	**(952)**	**(65)**	**(83)**

but as far as domestic work was concerned there was little difference according to employment situation (Table 22).

A comparatively high number of unhappy marriages (one in five among both mothers and fathers) were reported by parents in single earner households in which the *mother* was the only adult in the labour force, as well as by those, especially mothers, in *no earner* families. There was also a tendency for more disagreement over child-rearing and domestic tasks to be reported by parents in households with no adult in the labour force, and in those in which the mother was the sole earner. We saw earlier that these families were likely to be financially disadvantaged, to enjoy fewer activities together which involved expenditure, and that in neither case did unemployed fathers make a major contribution to domestic work or child care. It would seem from all these findings that the economic hardship and personal stress likely to be experienced in both situations puts considerable pressure upon the marital relationship.

The number of hours parents worked did not appear, in itself, to be linked to feelings about their marriage relationships (Table 23), or to consensus about bringing up children (Table 5.4). There was some variation, however, in relation to harmony over domestic work, with fathers employed for longer (50+) hours reporting *less* agreement with their wives, while for mothers working long (35+) hours was associated with

greater consensus (Table 24). This would seem to link with the trend noted in Chapter 3 for fathers' domestic contribution to fall as their own working hours increased, while mothers working long hours reported higher levels of shared housework.

For mothers, the most important factor relating to their marital happiness and consensus with their partner was the extent to which husbands were involved with the children. More than one in five mothers (22%) whose husbands did not contribute to the care and socialisation of children said that they were unhappy in their relationship, compared with just 7% of those in households in which these tasks were shared (Table 5.1). For mothers in employment, the proportion with uninvolved husbands reporting unhappy relationships rose in line with their own working hours, from 20% among those employed for less than 16 hours to 39% among those working 35+hours (Table 23).

The level of fathers' involvement with children was again the most important discriminating factor in relation to the levels of consensus reported by mothers. Only a third of those with uninvolved husbands indicated close agreement between the couple about child-rearing, and 9% said they frequently disagreed – three times as many as those whose husbands were involved in both child care and behaviour (Table 5.2). More than a quarter of the mothers with uninvolved husbands reported frequent disagreement over domestic work, compared with just 5% among

Table 22 Consensus with partner about sharing household tasks, by couple's employment situation

cohort fathers:	dual earner:		single earner:		no
	wife ft	wife pt	wife home	wife works	earner
	%	%	%	%	%
always agree	25	20	20	25	34
often agree	34	39	35	34	27
sometimes agree	30	29	33	23	22
often/always disagree	11	11	10	18	17
never talk about	<1	1	1	-	-
total	**100**	**100**	**100**	**100**	**100**
(n)	**(398)**	**(990)**	**(1010)**	**(44)**	**(77)**

cohort mothers:	dual earner:		single earner:		no
	mother ft	mother pt	mother home	mother works	earner
	%	%	%	%	%
always agree	28	22	26	20	18
often agree	33	31	30	26	34
sometimes agree	24	33	28	42	28
often/always disagree	13	13	13	12	16
never talk about	2	1	3	-	4
total	**100**	**100**	**100**	**100**	**100**
(n)	**(536)**	**(1255)**	**(951)**	**(65)**	**(82)**

Table 23 **Rating of marital relationship by father's involvement with children and hours worked**

a) Fathers	father's involvement:		b) Mothers	husband's involvement:	
30 - 39 hours:	high	low	**under 16 hours:**	high	low
unhappy (1-4)	11	10	unhappy (1-4)	2	20
5	9	12	5	8	18
6	35	34	6	27	34
happy (7)	45	44	happy (7)	63	28
total	**100**	**100**	**total**	**100**	**100**
(n)	**(163)**	**(41)**	**(n)**	**(79)**	**(61)**
40-49 hours:			**16-23 hours:**		
unhappy (1-4)	6	2	unhappy (1-4)	9	24
5	5	21	5	8	5
6	32	42	6	26	37
happy 7	57	35	happy 7	57	35
total	**100**	**100**	**total**	**100**	**100**
(n)	**(166)**	**(43)**	**(n)**	**(110)**	**(38)**
50-59 hours:			**24-34 hours:**		
unhappy (1-4)	11	10	unhappy (1-4)	8	32
5	4	6	5	9	11
6	31	32	6	28	36
happy 7	53	52	happy 7	55	21
total	**100**	**100**	**total**	**100**	**100**
(n)	**(45)**	**(31)**	**(n)**	**(71)**	**(28)**
60+ hours:			**60+ hours:**		
unhappy (1-4)	17	6	unhappy (1-4)	11	39
5	7	15	5	4	28
6	20	27	6	33	11
happy 7	56	52	happy 7	53	22
total	**100**	**100**	**total**	**100**	**100**
(n)	**(41)**	**(33)**	**(n)**	**(139)**	**(18)**

those with highly involved partners (Table 5.3). As with their ratings of their marital relationship, the longer the mothers' own working hours, the greater the discrepancy became: among those working 35+ hours a week, 39% with uninvolved husbands often or nearly always disagreed over housework, compared with just 5% of those whose partners were highly involved (Table 24). All of these findings would seem to indicate that the stress which many mothers experience in coping with the demands of both employment and family life is reflected in their relationship with a partner whose own contribution does little to alleviate it.

In marked contrast to the mothers, fathers' involvement with their children appeared to have very little connection with their own assessments of their marital relationship; interestingly, what difference there was went in the opposite direction to the pattern for mothers. The highest number of unhappy relationships was found among the most highly involved fathers (i.e. those sharing both child care and socialisation), and this tendency was particularly pronounced among those working long (60+) hours; 17% admitted they were unhappily married compared with just

6% of those who were least involved with their children (Table 23).

A rather different picture emerged with regard to areas of consensus. The fathers who were least involved with their children were twice as likely to report disagreements over domestic tasks as their highly involved counterparts (17% and 7% respectively, Table 5.3), and similar differences emerged in relation to child-rearing (Table 5.2). Unlike mothers, however, there was no consistent trend for disagreement to increase in line with fathers' working hours (Table 5.4). It could be that non-involvement among fathers working relatively short hours is as likely to produce friction as it is among those whose long hours may 'excuse' their low contribution to family tasks.

Happiness and satisfaction with life

As a further indicator of the cohort members' feelings of well-being or otherwise, they were asked *how satisfied they were with the way their lives had turned out so far,* placing themselves on a scale of 0 (completely dissatisfied) to 10 (completely satisfied). In order to simplify the findings, the responses were grouped into three:

Table 24 Consensus about domestic work by cohort members' working hours and level of fathers' involvement with children

a) Fathers 30-39 hours:	father's involvement: high %	low %	b) Mothers under 16 hours:	husband's involvement: high %	low %
nearly always agree	25	17	nearly always agree	31	11
often agree	41	39	often agree	36	29
sometimes agree	17	26	sometimes agree	28	33
often disagree	6	17	often disagree	6	22
never talk about	<1	—	never talk about	—	4
total	100	100	total	100	100
(n)	(189)	(46)	(n)	(87)	(72)
40-49 hours:			**16-23 hours:**		
nearly always agree	27	18	nearly always agree	25	18
often agree	42	37	often agree	39	11
sometimes agree	23	37	sometimes agree	32	41
often disagree	7	8	often disagree	4	27
never talk about	<1	—	never talk about	—	2
total	100	100	total	100	100
(n)	(193)	(51)	(n)	(122)	(44)
50-59 hours:			**23-24 hours:**		
nearly always agree	27	12	nearly always agree	39	6
often agree	33	38	often agree	38	23
sometimes agree	31	24	sometimes agree	16	36
often disagree	9	26	often disagree	4	36
never talk about	—	—	never talk about	3	—
total	100	100	total	100	100
(n)	(55)	(34)	(n)	(79)	(31)
60+ hours:			**35+ hours:**		
nearly always agree	33	11	nearly always agree	40	13
often agree	35	30	often agree	32	30
sometimes agree	28	43	sometimes agree	22	17
often disagree	5	13	often disagree	5	39
never talk about	—	5	never talk about	1	—
total	100	100	total	100	100
(n)	(43)	(37)	(n)	(163)	(23)

dissatisfied (0-6), fairly satisfied (7-8) and highly satisfied (9-10). Overall, mothers were more likely than fathers to indicate high satisfaction (34% and 24% respectively), although the proportions indicating dissatisfaction were similar (15% and 14%) (Table 5.5).

Looking at the couple's employment situation showed that, as with marital happiness, the highest level of satisfaction was expressed by fathers and mothers in the 'traditional' single earner families with employed fathers and home-based mothers, although, again, they differed only slightly from those in dual earner households (Table 25). In the latter group, there was no difference according to whether the mother/wife worked full- or part-time.

In contrast, both fathers and mothers in single earner families in which only the mother was in the labour market contained much higher proportions who were dissatisfied (28% and 22% respectively), while the highest level of discontent was expressed by fathers (39%) and mothers

(30%) in no earner families.

As with the ratings of their marital relationship, paternal involvement with children was a key factor in life satisfaction, especially for mothers. Dissatisfaction was more than twice as high (28%) among those with uninvolved husbands as among mothers whose partners contributed to all aspects of child-rearing (13%) (Table 5.5). When this was examined according to the number of hours worked by mothers who were employed, the variation was even more striking. The level of dissatisfaction among those with uninvolved husbands increased from 26% among those working less than 16 hours to 46% in the group working 35+ hours (Table 26).

Again, fathers' satisfaction with their lives varied little according to their involvement with their children, although, interestingly, the slight differences which did emerge were once more in the opposite direction to those among mothers. The highest proportion (16%) of dissatisfied fathers was found among those most involved,

Table 25   Satisfaction with life so far, by couple's employment situation

cohort fathers:		dual earner:		single earner:		no
		wife ft	wife pt	wife home	wife works	earner
		%	%	%	%	%
dissatisfied	(0-6)	15	15	10	28	39
	(7,8)	62	62	64	53	37
satisfied	(9,10)	23	23	26	19	24
total		**100**	**100**	**100**	**100**	**100**
(n)		**(399)**	**(992)**	**(1007)**	**(43)**	**(79)**

cohort mothers:		dual earner:		single earner:		no
		mother ft	mother pt	mother home	mother works	earner
		%	%	%	%	%
dissatisfied	(0-6)	16	14	13	22	30
	(7,8)	51	53	48	56	44
satisfied	(9,10)	33	33	38	22	26
total		**100**	**100**	**100**	**100**	**100**
(n)		**(531)**	**(1256)**	**(949)**	**(63)**	**(80)**

while the lowest proportion (11%) appeared among the uninvolved (Table 5.5). Fathers who worked very long (60+) hours and were also involved in both the care and behaviour of their children constituted the highest proportion expressing dissatisfaction: 21%, compared with 11% among similarly long-working fathers who were uninvolved with their children (Table 26).

Two further questions asked the cohort members where they would have placed themselves on the same scale of satisfaction ten years previously, and also where they expected to be in ten years' time. Overall, both fathers and mothers appeared to be much happier currently than they were in their early 20s (Table 5.5), and both groups also expected to enjoy greater satisfaction in their future lives. What was particularly striking, however, was that the current marked difference among mothers according to their husband's involvement with

Table 26   Satisfaction with life so far, by hours worked and fathers' involvement with children

a) Fathers 30-39 hours:		father's involvement in:		b) Mothers under 16 hours:		husband's involvement:	
		high	low			high	low
	%	%			%	%	
dissatisfied	(0-6)	16	14	dissatisfied	(0-6)	6	26
	(7,8)	62	71		(7,8)	48	54
satisfied	(9,10)	22	15	satisfied	(9,10)	56	19
total		**100**	**100**	**total**		**100**	**100**
(n)		**(189)**	**(47)**	**(n)**		**(87)**	**(72)**
40-49 hours:				**16-23 hours:**			
dissatisfied	(0-6)	8	6	dissatisfied	(0-6)	11	31
	(7,8)	64	67		(7,8)	48	47
satisfied	(9,10)	28	27	satisfied	(9,10)	41	22
total		**100**	**100**	**total**		**100**	**100**
(n)		**(191)**	**(51)**	**(n)**		**(121)**	**(45)**
50-59 hours:				**24-34 hours:**			
dissatisfied	(0-6)	14	15	dissatisfied	(0-6)	17	33
	(7,8)	64	68		(7,8)	46	53
satisfied	(9,10)	22	18	satisfied	(9,10)	37	13
total		**100**	**100**	**total**		**100**	**100**
(n)		**(55)**	**(34)**	**(n)**		**(78)**	**(30)**
60+ hours:				**35+ hours:**			
dissatisfied	(0-6)	21	11	dissatisfied	(0-6)	12	46
	(7,8)	56	57		(7,8)	52	42
satisfied	(9,10)	23	32	satisfied	(9,10)	36	12
total		**100**	**100**	**total**		**100**	**100**
(n)		**(43)**	**(37)**	**(n)**		**(162)**	**(24)**

children disappeared in their assessment of their past satisfaction. Looking ten years ahead, however, it re-appeared: those with non-contributing husbands were less likely than their peers with more involved partners to see themselves as very satisfied in the future. These findings reinforce the view that their partner's contribution was critical to mothers' current happiness in their relationship and general sense of well-being; it is also disturbing that some of those who were adversely affected by a lack of such support did not see an amelioration of their situation in the future. By contrast, although the differences among fathers were slight, it was those currently *least* involved with their children who had the most optimistic expectations of their own futures.

Given the very different perspectives held by fathers and mothers which these findings indicate, it was also interesting to note their responses to a question about locus of control. The great majority (over 90%) of both sexes indicated that they felt they could *'usually run my life as I want to'* (Table 5.6). However, mothers were, overall, more than twice as likely as fathers to say that they *'usually find life's problems too much'*, and those whose husbands were uninvolved in either the care and behaviour of their children were nearly four times more likely to express this view than those with highly involved partners (15% and 4% respectively). For fathers, the opposite was the case: those who contributed equally to family responsibilities were more than three times as likely to feel overwhelmed by life as their uninvolved counterparts (6% versus 2%).

Psychological distress

Finally, we examine the scores recorded by the NCDS parents on the Malaise Inventory. This is a 24-item checklist of symptoms, including anxiety, irritability, and depressed mood (Rutter *et al.*, 1970). A score of seven or more positive answers is generally taken to indicate that the person concerned is vulnerable to anxiety or depression.

It is well-established that women are more vulnerable than men to psychological distress (Bebbington *et al.*, 1991). The responses of the parents in our study confirmed this pattern, with twice as many mothers as fathers scoring seven or more (10% and 5% respectively: Table 5.7).

Taking the couples' employment circumstances into account showed that as many as one in three mothers in the no earner families appeared to be vulnerable to anxiety or depression (Table 27). By contrast, those who were the *sole* earners in their households did not differ in this respect from their peers in dual earner families or home-based mothers with employed husbands. Thus, despite the economic disadvantage of families in which only the mother was employed, and the relationship difficulties which were reported above, they were clearly less vulnerable than their counterparts in no earner households. It may be that the social and psychological benefits of employment are particularly salient to mothers with unemployed partners, and that, for them, these outweigh the mostly slight economic gains identified in Chapter 2.

Among the employed mothers overall, there was no consistent link between their working

Table 27	**Cohort member's malaise score, by couple's employment situation**				
cohort fathers:	**dual earner:**		**single earner:**		**no**
	wife ft	**wife pt**	**wife home**	**wife works**	**earner**
	%	%	%	%	%
7 or more (depressed)	5	4	4	13	17
under 7 (not depressed)	95	96	96	87	83
total	**100**	**100**	**100**	**100**	**100**
(n)	**(428)**	**(1046)**	**(1068)**	**(46)**	**(86)**
cohort mothers:	**dual earner:**		**single earner:**		**no**
	mother ft	**mother pt**	**mother home**	**mother works**	**earner**
	%	%	%	%	%
7 or more (depressed)	9	9	9	9	32
under 7 (not depressed)	91	91	91	91	68
total	**100**	**100**	**100**	**100**	**100**
(n)	**(563)**	**(1291)**	**(69)**	**(987)**	**(96)**

hours and their scores on the Malaise Inventory (Table 5.8). What *was* important for mothers generally, as has been the case for all the parent outcomes examined, was their husband's involvement with children. Mothers whose partners played little part in either child care or socialisation were rather more likely to have high malaise scores (13%) than those in other situations (9%) (Table 5.9).

Among the fathers, the picture was different: those who were out of the labour market were much more likely to have scores of seven or more, regardless of whether or not their wives were themselves in employment (13% and 17% respectively, compared with just 4% to 5% among employed fathers: Table 27). As far as employed fathers were concerned, there were no differences according to their wives' employment situation. However, working very long hours *was*

associated with low mood among fathers: one in ten of those working 60 or more hours a week had a score of seven or more, compared with less than one in 20 among those in all other working hours categories (Table 5.8).

Their employment status and working hours appeared to be the key factors affecting fathers' mental/emotional well-being. As with the other parental outcomes we have examined, their involvement with their children was not related in any way to their own emotional state (Table 5.9). These findings confirm our earlier conclusions that the circumstances of family life, in particular the contribution made by their partners, are critical for mothers' happiness and well-being; whereas the emotive perceptions of fathers are much less bound up with their own involvement in the family domain.

Conclusions

Successful parenting requires adequate resources. Among the most important are sufficient income to provide a satisfactory material environment, time, and the personal qualities appropriate to meeting children's needs for emotional security, stability and affection. The findings of this study have revealed wide disparities regarding the first two of these among a large sample of 33-year-old mothers and fathers in Britain in the early 1990s.

For most families, their economic situation and the time available for children and family life were structured by the relationship of one or both parents to the labour market. The actual employment position of the mothers and fathers studied reflected the polarisation into 'work rich' and 'work poor' households which has occurred in recent years, and the sharply different characteristics of each. Couples who were both in full-time employment tended to be better qualified and to have higher status occupations, while at the other end of the spectrum families with both parents out of the labour force were more likely to have no educational qualifications, and to have previously held low status jobs.

The contrasts in the economic resources of the different employment groups were striking. Families with two full-time earners were concentrated at the upper end of the household income distribution, indicating that two well-paid jobs, rather than simply two earners, are increasingly necessary to achieve satisfactory living standards. At the opposite end of the scale, the study highlighted the economic disadvantage suffered by families with no adult in employment (and also by those in which the mother was the sole earner). Since these families tended to be comparatively large, a disproportionate number of children were affected by the adverse consequences of parental exclusion from the labour force.

A key theme running through this study is that of parenting time. This resource, too, is closely linked to the relationship of parental couples to the labour market. A major focus of the analyses described in the preceding chapters has been the variation in parenting roles and family lives according to the employment situation of the couples in the study, and the time spent on work outside the home.

The most egalitarian parenting and domestic arrangements were found in households in which both parents were in full-time employment. Fathers in such families were more likely than their counterparts in other situations to play an equal part with their wives in child care, child-rearing and domestic work. It is important to stress, however, that the differences were relative, and that even in families with two full-time earners, mothers retained disproportionate responsibility for these areas of family life.

Fathers' family contribution appeared to be governed not only by their wives' employment situation, but also by the circumstances of their own paid work. Those who worked long or unsocial hours – and they were in the majority – tended to play correspondingly less part in child care and domestic work, even when their wives were also employed full-time. For fathers, therefore, it appeared that heavy work commitments outside the home represented an obstacle to equal parenting, and, as such, a source of conflicting pressures, particularly in families in which both parents were in full-time employment.

Most mothers, by contrast, worked relatively short hours. Many also worked at times – in the evenings, early mornings or weekends – when their husbands were likely to be available to look after the children. This would seem to suggest that, while fathers' employment situations set the framework for their domestic contribution, for mothers, family life and its related responsibilities were decisive factors influencing their involvement in the labour force.

Thus, as other studies have shown, despite the sharp increase in the labour market participation of mothers during the period in which these 33-year-olds made the transitions to employment and parenthood, there remained a significant degree of gender segregation in the way in which their respective parenting roles were undertaken.

What was less easy to discern was the extent to which different influences operated to sustain these divisions. Were fathers constrained by financial pressures, or increasingly pervasive job insecurity, to work long hours, or did they opt to do so, seeing their employment role as central to their own aspirations and satisfactions? How far was mothers' labour market participation limited by the employment opportunities available to them, and the lack of provision for child care, and to what extent did mothers choose to undertake particular jobs – or to remain out of the labour force altogether – to enable them to undertake a caring role which they perceived as of primary importance?

Nor do we know whether couples had explicitly negotiated their respective employment and family roles. The great majority of the parents studied appeared highly contented with their marital relationships and their lives in general: those in 'traditional' families, in which only the father was in employment, were marginally the most satisfied of all. The study's data concerning the division of paid work, domestic labour and child-rearing tasks between these couples indicated that they were the group which had adopted, and seemingly accepted, the most segregated parenting roles. Such positive perceptions are consistent with those of other investigations, especially as far as mothers are concerned. It has been noted elsewhere that inequalities in actual partnerships may be viewed very differently from attitudes to gender roles in general, and that women express little overt dissatisfaction at their disproportionate responsibility in the domestic arena, seeing this as part of the 'natural order of things' (Brannen and Moss, 1991; Henwood et al., 1987).

We also found, however, a sizeable minority of parents – especially mothers – who were *not* happy with their marriage relationship or their overall lives, and a smaller group who indicated signs of psychological distress. For mothers, the key factor in these outcomes appeared to be their partner's contribution – or rather the lack of it – to family life and the tasks of parenting. The greatest discontent was expressed by mothers who themselves were employed for long hours, indicating the stress and, it would seem, resentment produced by undertaking what were effectively two full-time jobs. It must also be pointed out, however, that unhappiness relating to their husband's non-involvement was not confined to employed mothers, thus emphasising the importance for mothers generally of the father's role in family life.

For fathers, on the other hand, involvement or otherwise in the care and socialisation of their children seemed to have little bearing on their marital happiness, general life satisfaction or emotional state. Indeed, there was even some indication that fathers who were said to be playing an equal part in the care of their children were the least content in these respects. This suggests that these fathers, like the mothers who expressed dissatisfaction, were experiencing the pressures and strains of a demanding role both at work and at home, although for fathers, of course, family responsibilities involved a shared commitment, while the mothers concerned were shouldering the domestic burden alone.

It is clear from the findings of this study that the factors influencing the employment and domestic roles adopted by parental couples, and their feelings about these roles, are numerous and complex. They are located in both the public domain of the economic and social fabric of our society and also in the private world of individual attitudes and values. As a consequence, the study's findings have implications for policy measures and interventions to support successful parenting which range from employment practice and child-care provision to personal development and education for family life.

There are a number of employment issues which are clearly of crucial importance for parenting resources. As this study has shown, parental disconnection from the labour market, or reliance on earnings from part-time work, do not provide an adequate basis for the economic support of dependent children. The most economically disadvantaged families in our study were those in which both parents were unemployed, or the mother was the sole, usually part-time, earner. Since 1991, when the NCDS survey was carried out, the number of women *and men* in part-time jobs has increased each year, while the number in full-time employment has declined (*Employment Gazette*, April 1995). It is also important to note that the proportion of employees working part-time because they could not find full-time jobs rose from 6% in 1990 to 13% in 1993 (*Employment Gazette*, December 1994). Such trends suggest that the relative disadvantage suffered by many of the families in our study is likely to have intensified since the survey took place.

Our findings also showed that the long hours worked by most of the fathers in the study were associated with a detachment from family life and parenting responsibilities. Here, too, most recent trends indicate a further increase in the time spent at work. Since 1991, as the economic recovery has progressed, employers have tended to lengthen the hours of those already in post before taking on new staff (Central Statistical Office, 1995).

The growth in part-time work, the increase in working hours, and other recent trends such as the moves toward short and fixed-term contracts and casualised employment, are all features of the 'flexible' labour market which has affected every occupational sector. In their aims they are essentially geared to the competitive interests of employers and the economy, rather than to the needs and wishes of family members (e.g. Simkin and Hillage, 1992). As Land (1995) has pointed out, 'it would be wrong to assume that the growth of part-time work is a response to women's pressure to combine paid work with child care'. In practice, these trends are likely to be antipathetic to family life, in their effect upon family finances and the time available for both parents and children to be together.

As other writers (e.g. Brannen, 1994) have noted, what is needed is more 'family friendly' employment practices to counter the negative impact of so many recent trends. Practices which recognise the family responsibilities of workers and, most importantly, those of fathers as well as mothers, would ameliorate a situation in which commitment to the labour market is an obstacle to effective parenting. The most frequently cited measures relate to parental leave, to *paternity* as well as maternity leave, to the need for career breaks, and so on. However, the findings of this study also suggest that the negative impact on family life of the long hours which most fathers spend at work make this an issue requiring urgent consideration.

The other side of the employment coin for parents with young children is the issue of child care. This study has highlighted once again the very minor role played by public provision in this area, and the reliance of working parents on the family itself, and other informal sources, for the care of their children. The arrangements reported by many of the parents in this study indicated that employed mothers had adopted hours of work which enabled their partners to look after the children. It is likely that, under these constraints, mothers had very little choice of employment, and were limited to low status and poorly paid work. Such narrow options are not conducive to meeting the economic needs of families, or to enabling mothers to maintain, or acquire, marketable skills and financial independence in a context of increasing instability in family life. More widely available and affordable child-care

provision would go a long way towards removing such constraints (Ward et al., 1994).

'Family friendly' employment practices and appropriate child-care provision have a vital role to play in giving all parents meaningful choices in how they arrange their parenting roles. However, creating a supportive economic and social framework for family life can be seen as a necessary, but not sufficient, condition for such options to be exercised. Our study has revealed marked discrepancies in the views and perceptions held by mothers and fathers of their respective roles, which may well persist in a social context which enables and encourages more egalitarian parenting behaviour. In Sweden, for example, the introduction of paternal leave has had to be followed by a campaign to persuade fathers to avail themselves of the provision (Bjornberg, 1994).

There is thus a further policy issue which is of relevance here. This concerns the importance of preparing young people for adult relationships and parenthood in the increasingly complex and diverse contexts in which these will take place. The prevailing social policy ethos emphasises parents' private responsibility for the care and upbringing of their children. In effect, this equates with a high degree of parental *autonomy,* rather than collectively recognised *obligations*: our society shows little active concern for how parents tackle their role unless children's welfare is perceived to be at risk (Land and Parker, 1978). Yet raising the next generation in today's society is probably more difficult and unsupported than at any previous period, and it is vital that young people are adequately prepared and equipped for the complexities and responsibilities of parenthood.

This is not a new idea, and in recent years a number of interesting developments have taken place in this area (Pugh et al., 1994). However, a more explicit and universal commitment is required, which can only be achieved by giving preparation for family life a central place in mainstream education through the national curriculum. The current focus throughout the education system on academic and vocational achievement is in no way matched by a voiced concern for the development of social, communication and relationship skills. Yet, given the diversity of arrangements that characterise family life in Britain today, the success of the relationships involved will depend more than ever upon an awareness, and negotiated acceptance, of each others' experiences, expectations, and aspirations.

References

Bebbington, P. E., Hurry, J. and Tennant, C. (1991). The Camberwell Community Survey: a summary of results. *Social Psychiatry and Psychiatric Epidemiology*, 26, 195-201.

Belsky, J. (1984). The determinants of parenting: a process model. *Child Development*, 55, 83-96.

Bimbi, F. (1992). Parenthood in Italy: assymetric relationships and family affection. In Bjornberg, U., *European parents in the 1990s: contradictions and comparisons*. New Brunswick and London: Transaction Publishers.

Bjornberg, U. (ed.) (1992). *European parents in the 1990s: contradictions and comparisons*. New Brunswick and London: Transaction Publishers.

Bjornberg, U. (1994). Reconciling family and employment in Sweden. In Letablier, M.-T. and Hantrais, L. (Eds.), Cross-National Research Papers no. 2: *The family-employment relationship*. ESRC/CNAF.

Bjornberg, U. (1995). Family orientations among men: fatherhood and partnership in a process of change. In Brannen, J. and O'Brien, M. (Eds.), *Childhood and parenthood*. Proceedings of the International Sociological Association Committee for Family Research Conference, 1994.

Brannen, J. (1992). British parenthood in the wake of the New Right: some contradictions and changes. In Bjornberg, U. (Ed.), *European parents in the 1990s: contradictions and comparisons*. New Brunswick and London: Transaction Publishers.

Brannen, J. (1994). Sociological definitions of the family-employment relationship in the United Kingdom. In Letablier, M.-T. and Hantrais, L. (Eds.), Cross-National Research Papers no. 2: *The family-employment relationship*. ESRC/CNAF.

Brannen, J., Meszaros, G., Moss, P. and Poland, G. (1994). *Employment and family life: a review of research in the UK (1980-1994)*. Employment Department. London: HMSO.

Brannen, J. and Moss, P. (1988). *New mothers at work: employers and children*. London: Unwin Hyman.

Brannen, J. and Moss, P. (1991). *Managing mothers: dual earner households after maternity leave*. London: Macmillan.

Bridgwood, A. and Savage, P. (1993). *General Household Survey 1991*. London: HMSO.

Butler, N. R. and Bonham, D. G. (1963). *Perinatal mortality*. Edinburgh: Livingstone.

Bynner, J. and Fogelman, K. (1993). Making the grade: education and training experiences. In Ferri, E. (Ed.), *Life at 33: the fifth follow-up of the National Child Development Study*. London: National Children's Bureau and City University.

Bynner, J. and Steedman, J. (1995). *Difficulties with basic skills: findings from the 1970 British Cohort Study*. London: The Basic Skills Agency.

Carlsen, S. and Larsen, J. E. (Eds.) (1994). *The equality dilemma*. Copenhagen: Danish Equal Status Council.

Central Statistical Office (1995). *Labour Market Trends*, December. London: HMSO.

Cohen, B. (1988). *Caring for children: report for the European Commission's Childcare Network*. London: Commission of the European Communities.

Condy, A. and Roberts, C. (1995). Appendix 3: FPSC: Families and work briefing. In Proceedings of seminars 27 and 31 October 1994. London: Family Policy Studies Centre.

Davie, R., Butler, N. and Goldstein, H. (1972). *From birth to seven*. London: Longman in association with National Children's Bureau.

Dex, S., Clark, A. and Taylor, M. (1993). Household labour supply. Report from ESRC Centre on Micro-social Change, University of Essex.

Dobson, B., Beardsworth, A., Keil, T. and Walker, R. (1994). *Diet, choice and parenting: social, cultural and nutritional aspects of food consumption among low income families*. London: Family Policy Studies Centre/Joseph Rowntree Foundation.

Eekelaar, J. (1991). Parental responsibility: state of nature or nature of the state? *Journal of Social Welfare and Family Law*, no. 1, 37-50.

Employment Gazette (1994). December.

Employment Gazette (1995). April.

Etzioni, A. (1993). *The parenting deficit*. London: Demos.

European Commission Childcare Network (1993). *Mothers, fathers and employment 1985-1991*. Brussels: European Commission DG5.

European Community Directorate of Social Affairs (1993). *The Europeans and the family*. Eurobarometer 39. Brussels: European Commission DG5.

Eurostat (1992). *Labour force survey results, 1990*. Luxembourg: Office for Official Publications of the European Community.

Ferri, E. (1984). *Stepchildren: a national study*. Windsor: NFER-Nelson.

Ferri, E. (1992). *What makes childminding work?* London: National Children's Bureau.

Ferri, E. (Ed.) (1993). *Life at 33: the fifth follow-up of the National Child Development Study*. London: National Children's Bureau and City University.

Ferri, E. and Smith, K. (forthcoming (a)). Parenthood at 33: the fifth follow-up of the National Child Development Study. SSRU NCDS User Support Group Working Paper. London: City University.

Ferri, E. and Smith, K. (forthcoming (b)). Family breakdown and family conflict. SSRU NCDS User Support Group Working paper. London: City University.

Fogelman, K. (1976). *Britain's 16-year-olds*. London: National Children's Bureau.

Furstenberg, F. J. (1987). The new extended family: the experience of parents and children after remarriage. In Pasley, K. and Ihinger Tallman, M. (Eds.), *Remarriage and stepparents*. New York: Guilford Press.

Gershuny, J. (1995). Relationships between women's employment and other activities. In Bayley, R., Condy, A. and Roberts, C. (Eds.), *Policies for families: work, poverty and resources*. London: Family Policy Studies Centre.

Gershuny, J. and Jones, S. (1987). The changing work/leisure balance in Britain 1961-1984. *Sociological Review* Monograph, 33, 9-50.

Gittins, D. (1985). *The family in question*. London: Macmillan.

Gregg, P. and Wadsworth, J. (1995). More work in fewer households? In Hills, J. (Ed.), *New inequalities*. Cambridge: Cambridge University Press.

Gregson, N. and Lowe, M. (1993). Renegotiating the domestic division of labour? A study of dual career households in north-east and south-east England. *Sociological Review*, 41 (3), 475-504.

Harrop, A. and Moss, P. (1994). Working parents: trends in the 1980s. *Employment Gazette*, 102 (10), 343-52.

Henwood, M., Rimmer, L. and Wicks, M. (1987). *Inside the family*. London: Family Policy Studies Centre.

HMSO (1993). *General Household Survey 1991*.

HMSO (1994). *General Household Survey 1992*.

Kiernan, K. (1992). Men and women at work and at home. In Jowell, R., Brook, L., Prior, G. and Taylor, B. (Eds.), *British Social Attitudes: 9th Report*. Cambridge: Dartmouth.

Kiernan, K. (1995). Transition to parenthood: young mothers, young fathers: associated factors and later life experiences. STICERD Discussion paper WSP/113. London: London School of Economics.

Kiernan, K. and Estaugh, V. (1993). *Cohabitation: extra-marital childbearing and social policy*. London: Family Policy Studies Centre.

Kiernan, K. and Wicks, M. (1990). *Family change and future policy*. London: Family Policy Studies Centre/Joseph Rowntree Foundation.

Kumar, V. (1993). *Poverty and inequality in the UK: the effects on children*. London: National Children's Bureau.

Lamb, M. E. (Ed.) (1986). *The role of the father in child development*. New York: Wiley.

Lamb, M. E., Pleck, J. H. and Levine, J. A. (1987). In Lewis, C. and O'Brien, M. (Eds.), *Reassessing fatherhood*. London: Sage Publications.

Land, H. (1995). Paying for care. In Bayley, R., Condy, A. and Roberts, C. (Eds.), *Policies for families: work, poverty and resources*. London: Family Policy Studies Centre.

Land, H. and Parker, R. (1978). United Kingdom. In Kamerman, S. B. and Kahn, A. J. (Eds.), *Family policy: government and family in 14 countries*. New York: Columbia University Press.

Lewis, C. (1987). The observation of father–infant relationships: an 'attachment' to outmoded concepts. In McKee, L. and O'Brien, M. (Eds.), *The father figure*. London: Tavistock Publications.

Lewis, C., Newson, E. and Newson, J. (1982). Father participation through childhood and its relationship with career aspirations and delinquency. In Beail, N. and McGuire, J. (Eds.), *Fathers: psychological perspectives*. London: Junction Books.

Lewis, S. N. and Cooper, C. L. (1988). Stress in dual earner families. *Women at Work*, 3, 139-68.

McRae, S. (1993 (a)). Returning to work after childbirth: opportunities and inequalities. *European Sociological Review*, 9, 125-38.

McRae, S. (1993 (b)). *Cohabiting mothers*. London: Policy Studies Institute.

McRae, S. and Daniel, W.W. (1991). *Maternity rights in Britain: first findings*. London: Policy Studies Institute.

Macran, S., Joshi, H. and Dex, S. (1995). Employment after childbearing: a survival analysis. SSRU NCDS User Support Group Working Paper no. 40. London: City University.

Marsh, A. and McKay, S. (1993). Families, work and the use of childcare. *Employment Gazette*, 101 (8), 361-70.

Martin, J. and Roberts, C. (1984). *Women and employment: a lifetime perspective*. London: HMSO.

Moss, P. (1990). Work, family and the care of children: issues of equality and responsibility. *Children and Society*, 4, 2.

Moxnes, K. (1992). Changes in family patterns: changes in parenting? In Bjornberg, U. (Ed.), *European parents in the 1990s: contradictions and comparisons*. New Brunswick and London: Transaction Publishers.

O'Brien, M. (1982). The working father. In Beail, N. and McGuire, J. (Eds.), *Fathers: psychological perspectives*. London: Junction Books.

O'Brien, M. (1992). Changing conceptions of fatherhood. In Bjornberg, U. (Ed.), *European parents in the 1990s: contradictions and comparisons*. New Brunswick and London: Transaction Publishers.

Oechsle, M. and Zoll, R. (1992). Young people and their ideas on parenthood. In Bjornberg, U. (Ed.), *European parents in the 1990s: contradictions and comparisons*. New Brunswick and London: Transaction Publishers.

Office of Population Censuses and Surveys (1994a). *1991 Census: household and family composition*. London: HMSO.

Office of Population Censuses and Surveys (1994b). *1992 General Household Survey*. London: HMSO.

Pahl, R. (1984). *Divisions of labour.* Oxford: Blackwell.

Payne, J. (1987). Does unemployment run in families? Some findings from the GHS. *Sociology,* 21, 199-214.

Pelz, M. (1992). Living with children: desire and reality. In Bjornberg, U. (Ed.), *European parents in the 1990s: contradictions and comparisons.* New Brunswick and London: Transaction Publishers.

Petersen, H. (1994). Law and order in family life and working life. In Carlsen, S. and Larsen, J.E. (Eds.), *The equality dilemma.* Copenhagen: Danish Equal Status Council.

Pugh, G., De'ath, E. and Smith, C. (1994). *Confident parents, confident children: policy and practice in parent education and support.* London: National Children's Bureau.

Rutter, M., Tizard, J. and Whitmore, W. (1970). *Education, health and behaviour.* London: Longman.

Simkin, C. and Hillage, J. (1992). *Family friendly working: new hope or old hype?* IMS Report 224. Brighton: Institute of Manpower Studies.

Social Trends 1994. London: HMSO.

Sweeting, H. and West, P. (1995). Family life and health in adolescence: a role for culture in the health inequalities debate? *Social Science Medicine,* 40, 2, 163-75.

Utting, D. (1995) *Family and parenthood: supporting families, preventing breakdown.* York: Joseph Rowntree Foundation.

Ward, C., Dale, A. and Joshi, H. (1994). Combining employment with childcare: an escape from dependence? SSRU NCDS User Support Group Working Paper no. 38. London: City University.

Warde, A. and Hetherington, K. (1993). A changing domestic division of labour? Issues of measurement and interpretation. *Work, Employment and Society,* 7 (1), 23-45.

Wedge, P. (1969). The second follow-up of the National Child Development Study. *Concern,* no. 3, 34-9.

Wheelock, J. (1990). *Husbands at home: the domestic economy in a post-industrial society.* London: Routledge.

Working for Childcare (1990). *Meeting the childcare challenge: can the market provide?.* London: Working for Childcare.

00204221

To: Family Policy Studies Centre, 9 Tavistock Place, London WC1H 9SN

Telephone: 0207 388 5900   Fax: 0207 388 5600

Please send me the following publications

Title	Price	Quantity	Total
Diet, choice and poverty	£7.50		
Excluding primary school children	£9.50		
Family support for young people	£7.50		
Nutrition and diet in lone-parent families in London	£9.50		
Young single mothers: barriers to independent living	£9.50		
Single lone mothers: problems, prospects and policies	£9.50		
Dependence and independence in the finances of women aged 33	£9.50		
Learning to be a parent: a survey of group-based parenting programmes	£9.50		
The employment of lone parents: a comparison of policy in 20 countries	£9.50		
Small change: the impact of the Child Support Act on lone mothers and children	£9.50		
Family obligations in Europe	£9.50		
Parenting in the 1990s	£9.50		

Please add p&p as follows:
UK orders: £5.01–£15.00 add £1.50; £15.01–£25.00 add £3.00;
                 £25.01–£35.00 add £4.50; £35.01 & over add £6.00
Overseas orders: please request cost of p&p from FPSC
                 before sending sterling payment

Postage and packing	
Total	

☐ **I enclose a cheque/PO payable to FPSC for £** _____

☐ **Please invoice me (and indicate if invoice and delivery address differ)**

Name _____

Address _____

_____

_____

_____

_____

☐ Please send me the Centre's latest publications list

Family & Parenthood
Policy & Practice

PUBLISHED BY
Family Policy Studies Centre

SUPPORTED BY
JR JOSEPH ROWNTREE FOUNDATION

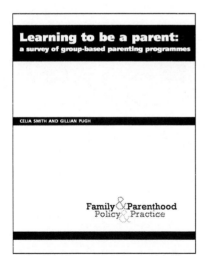

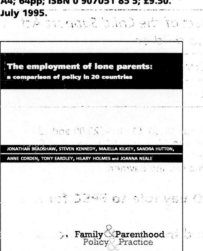

Nutrition and diet in lone-parent families in London
by Elizabeth Dowler and Claire Calvert.
This study asks whether nutritional deprivation is also a part of the poverty so generally experienced by lone parent families, and investigates the strategies adopted by lone parents for making ends meet.
A4; 60pp; ISBN 0 907051 79 0; £9.50.
February 1995.

Young single mothers *by Suzanne Speak et al.*
This research, centred on the City of Newcastle upon Tyne, investigates the barriers to independent living, as experienced by young, single never-married mothers, setting up their first independent homes, without the financial or practical assistance of a partner.
A4; 64pp; ISBN 0 907051 85 5; £9.50.
July 1995.

Single lone mothers *by Louie Burghes with Mark Brown*
This report considers single, lone mothers – women who have never been married and who live alone with their dependent children. They are indistinguishable in statistics from those who have never cohabited, yet may have very different characteristics and circumstances. From a policy-making perspective, it is important to understand why.
A4; 72pp; ISBN 0 907051 84 7; £9.50.
November 1995.

Learning to be a parent *by Celia Smith and Gillian Pugh*
This report describes the findings of a survey of group-based parenting programmes, courses and materials throughout the UK. It finds parents enthusiastic about the programme, and puts forward policy recommendations for their development.
A4; 56pp; ISBN 0 907051 90 1; £9.50.
February 1996.

The employment of lone parents: a comparison of policy in 20 countries
by Jonathan Bradshaw et al.
Uses data from the 15 EU states, Norway, Australia, New Zealand, Japan and the USA to look at factors that encourage, and discourage, lone parents to work outside the home.
A4; 64pp; ISBN 0 907051 95 2; £9.50.
May 1996.

Family obligations in Europe
by Jane Millar and Andrea Warman
As family structures and employment patterns throughout Europe change dramatically how should the family and the state provide care and support? This study compares definitions of family obligations in law and policy in 16 countries: asking *who* is responsible for whom, and *what* are they responsible for?
A4; 56pp; ISBN 0 907051 97 9; £9.50.
November 1996.

Postage and packing: up to £5.00 **free**; £5.01 – £15.00 **add £1.50**; £15.01 – £25.00 **add £3.00**; £25.01 – £35.00 **add £4.50**; £35.01 & over **add £6.00**

Published and distributed by Family Policy Studies Centre, 9 Tavistock Place, London WC1H 9SN • Tel: 020 7388 5900 • Fax: 020 7388 5600

00204221

00204221